Christ's Empowering Presence p[...]
spiritual resources. The autho[...]
ers through the ages and at th[...]
heritage. This book will introduce readers to some useful writers that
have been neglected in recent writings in this area. His grounding of
the spiritual life in Colossians 3 provides both a solid biblical foundation and a helpful organizing structure for the entire book.

James Wilhoit, Ph.D.
Scripture Press Chair of Christian Formation & Ministry, Wheaton College
Author, *Dictionary of Biblical Imagery* and *Nurture That Is Christian*

I feel a great kinship with this volume. The history of the Vineyard
Churches has been and remains a pursuit of God's presence. There
are many things I love about Gary's book. In it you will find church
history, deep spirituality, and practicality. I always want to know how
something actually works! Best of all is that this book is written by a
fellow traveler on the Way. You can trust his map!

Lance Pittluck
Senior Pastor, Anaheim Vineyard
Western Regional Director of the Vineyard USA

Gary Tyra offers his readers a fine survey of what Scripture and
devotional writers, both ancient and modern, have to say about the
theme of the empowering presence of Christ. By means of extensive
quotation, he traces this foundational issue from the OT and NT on
through key writers in the medieval and reformation era up to this
present day, guided by the foundational insights of his mentor Dallas
Willard. Gary Tyra shares in a very personal and practical way how he
himself pursues on a daily basis this empowering presence of Christ.

Richard Peace, Ph.D.
Robert Boyd Munger Professor of Evangelism & Spiritual Formation
Fuller Theological Seminary

Abiding with Jesus each day is an invitation open to all. Gary Tyra is willing to be your guide to move into a more personally enriching relationship with Jesus. You'll benefit greatly from the many excerpts of both classic and contemporary formation literature regarding what such a relationship looks like. The book is encouraging, motivational, and very practical.

Klaus Issler
Professor of Christian Education and Theology
Talbot School of Theology, La Mirada, CA

Spiritual life involves keeping company with God. But how do we cultivate such experiences in this life? Relying on the wisdom of a few Christian spiritual masters, both classic and contemporary, Tyra ably and succinctly describes for us the ways that make up the way we find him and his life.

Eric L. Johnson, Ph.D.
Director, Society for Christian Psychology
Lawrence and Charlotte Hoover Professor of Pastoral Care
Southern Baptist Theological Seminary

The Christian life is an ever-deepening relationship of intimacy with Jesus Christ. In *Christ's Empowering Presence*, Gary Tyra provides a biblically rooted, historically rich, and personally honest guide to this journey. It provides a helpful and approachable illustration of the spiritual direction provided by Dallas Willard in his writings. If you find yourself hungry for a closer and more fruitful walk with God, this book will most certainly serve as a useful guide to help you on your way.

Alan Fadling
Associate Director and Journey Dean of Training
The Leadership Institute, Mission Viejo, CA

Gary is gripped by the real offer of the "with-God" life. This book can help you find that.

John Ortberg
Senior Pastor, Menlo Park Presbyterian Church
Author, *The Life You've Always Wanted* and *God Is Closer than You Think*

The empowering, interactive presence of God is not only the topic of this book, but it's somehow the atmosphere of this book. As you read it, you sense God's presence and begin to think: This is what everyone truly longs for!

Jan Johnson
Author, *When the Soul Listens* and *Abundant Simplicity*

CHRIST'S EMPOWERING PRESENCE

CHRIST'S EMPOWERING PRESENCE

The Pursuit of God through the Ages

GARY TYRA

 Transforming lives through God's Word

Transforming lives through God's Word

Biblica provides God's Word to people through translation, publishing and Bible engagement in Africa, Asia Pacific, Europe, Latin America, Middle East, and North America. Through its worldwide reach, Biblica engages people with God's Word so that their lives are transformed through a relationship with Jesus Christ.

Biblica Publishing
We welcome your questions and comments.
1820 Jet Stream Drive, Colorado Springs, CO 80921 USA
www.Biblica.com

Christ's Empowering Presence
ISBN-13: 978-1-60657-096-8

To Dallas Willard, whose writings, lectures, and personal example have affected my life and ministry in many significant ways. Thank you.

CONTENTS

ACKNOWLEDGMENTS

Having dedicated this work on Christian spirituality to my primary mentor in this matter—Dallas Willard—I want now to express my gratitude to a number of other individuals without whose help this book would have never been.

First, I owe a tremendous debt of thanks to the folks at Biblica Publishing: publisher Volney James, for believing in the project and giving it a green light; John Dunham, who in his role as editorial manager made sure the publication process ran smoothly; and Andy Sloan, who has become to me not just an editorial partner, but a long-distance friend.

Second, I would like to express my deep appreciation to all the contemporary spiritual life authors cited in this study (especially Dallas Willard, John Ortberg, and Jan Johnson), and to their publishers, for allowing me to make use of their work. The goal I had in mind—to write a book that might function for its readers as an ongoing spiritual life resource—would have been impossible to attempt, much less accomplish, had it not been for the generosity of these publishing colleagues.

Finally, I want to publicly thank my wife, Patti, who, as a gifted author in her own right, not only proofread my manuscript several times but also made significant contributions to its content. This is a better book because of her involvement with it.

Now that this work has been released to the world at large, my hope is that the people cited above will feel good about the role they played in helping make it happen. God bless you all!

INTRODUCTION

"You have formed us for yourself, and our heart is restless until it rests in you."[1] Historically, Christian ministers have used this famous quote from Saint Augustine's *Confessions* in order to evangelize—to convince highly secularized people of the need to pay attention to the spiritual side of their existence. However, it now appears that most of us living in what we used to consider the secularized nations of the world no longer require this prompting. Just a few years ago, *Newsweek* published a fascinating, eye-opening article entitled "In Search of the Spiritual." It described "a world of 'hungry people, looking for a deeper relationship with God,'" and made the point that within contemporary society "'spirituality,' the impulse to seek communion with the Divine, is thriving."[2]

Is this impulse to seek communion with the Divine at work in your life? Are you spiritually hungry, looking for a deeper relationship with God? If so, what kind of spirituality are you hoping to experience? What would you say if I told you of an approach to spiritual formation that can bring not only a powerful sense of existential peace into your heart but can also make it possible for you to become the kind of person that, deep down inside, you know God created you to be?

A "Colossians 3 kind of life"

"You know you want this!" During the latter portion of my three-decade-long career as a teaching pastor, I found myself uttering this phrase at the conclusion of many of my most challenging sermons. Having done my best to help my hearers understand the life implications of this or that passage of Scripture, I would then encourage them to view what was often a strong, challenging biblical exhortation as an exciting invitation to begin living in a more Christlike manner. "You know you want this. You know you were made for this. You know that deep inside you'd really like to be the type of Christ-follower who's capable of living in this God-pleasing manner!"

Over the years, I found that some biblical texts require this kind of sermonic "framing." Consider, for example, Colossians 3:5–17, a passage that contains an intimidating list of moral imperatives:

> Put to death, therefore, whatever belongs to your earthly nature: sexual immorality, impurity, lust, evil desires and greed, which is idolatry. Because of these, the wrath of God is coming. You used to walk in these ways, in the life you once lived. But now you must rid yourselves of all such things as these: anger, rage, malice, slander, and filthy language from your lips. Do not lie to each other, since you have taken off your old self with its practices and have put on the new self, which is being renewed in knowledge in the image of its Creator. Here there is no Greek or Jew, circumcised or uncircumcised, barbarian, Scythian, slave or free, but Christ is all, and is in all.
>
> Therefore, as God's chosen people, holy and dearly loved, clothe yourselves with compassion, kindness,

humility, gentleness and patience. Bear with each other and forgive whatever grievances you may have against one another. Forgive as the Lord forgave you. And over all these virtues put on love, which binds them all together in perfect unity.

Let the peace of Christ rule in your hearts, since as members of one body you were called to peace. And be thankful. Let the word of Christ dwell in you richly as you teach and admonish one another with all wisdom, and as you sing psalms, hymns and spiritual songs with gratitude in your hearts to God. And whatever you do, whether in word or deed, do it all in the name of the Lord Jesus, giving thanks to God the Father through him.

At first glance, this passage might appear to be nothing more than a formidable laundry list of onerous expectations that Paul placed on the poor Colossian Christians in a more or less impatient fashion. But let's take a closer look. Isn't it true that this passage also indicates that it's possible for sincere followers of Christ to live in ways that, deep inside, they've always dreamed of—to become people who

- are overcoming the power of sexual lust;
- feel no need to be greedy or stingy toward others;
- routinely speak the truth in love, rather than engaging in slippery speech;
- love others despite their idiosyncratic tendencies;
- perpetually experience the peace of Christ in their hearts;
- consistently function as peacemakers, rather than as troublemakers, within their circle of friends;
- are genuinely positive people—always ready, whatever their circumstances, to offer sincere thanksgiving to God?

These are just some of the new lifestyle possibilities Colossians 3 speaks to us about. I ask you: Who wouldn't want this? Who wouldn't want to believe that we might someday come to a place in our spiritual journey where it's possible to actually pull off these moral and spiritual imperatives—or at least to do a better job with them?

As I said, I believe I know the secret to being able to live in this remarkably satisfying manner. You see, the Christlike life described in Colossians 3:5–17 is prefaced by some important words of pastoral counsel in Colossians 3:1–4. This very important prelude reads this way:

> Since, then, you have been raised with Christ, set your hearts on things above, where Christ is seated at the right hand of God. Set your minds on things above, not on earthly things. For you died, and your life is now hidden with Christ in God. When Christ, who is your life, appears, then you also will appear with him in glory.

These words, so obviously rich in significance, are nevertheless a bit difficult to comprehend. It's apparent from their context that Paul was endeavoring to help his readers understand how they might forge something other than an ultimately frustrating manner of life earmarked by a seemingly insurmountable compulsion toward sensual indulgence (see Colossians 2:18–23). According to the apostle Paul, the Colossian Christians needed to shift their focus away from their own limited physical resources and train their attention instead on the person and power of the risen and ascended Jesus. This is the key to a more spiritually satisfying existence. Indeed, this is the key to achieving the Christlike kind of life Paul goes on to delineate in Colossians 3:5–17. *We must learn to experience a perpetual sense of the risen Christ's empowering presence, to live our lives each and every day drawing on the rich resources of the one who, having overcome all things (see John 16:33), presently abides at the right hand of God the Father in heaven!*

Corroboration for the Concept

I believe the experience of Christ's empowering presence is the key to our ability to do justice to Colossians 3:5–17. Supported by many biblical texts (which we will examine in due course), this concept is also corroborated in the writings of classic and contemporary experts on Christian spirituality, including my primary mentor on this topic, Dallas Willard, professor of philosophy at the University of Southern California and renowned author of several important works on Christian spirituality.

At the risk of greatly oversimplifying things, the heart of Willard's teaching on Christian discipleship lies in the startling assertion that Jesus wants to empower his followers—his apprentices—to learn to live the way he would if he were in their place.[3] The gospel or "good news" concerning the kingdom of God that Jesus proclaimed during his earthly ministry was not simply that our sins could be forgiven so that we can experience eternal life in an age to come (though he did teach this). No, the good news, according to Willard, is that it's possible, through faith and confidence in Jesus, for us to become a new kind of people, capable of living a new kind of life right here and right now!

Going further, Willard is convinced that the secret to our learning to live in a manner reminiscent of the virtues and values of God's kingdom is to imitate and obey Jesus in the practice of *spiritual disciplines*. The classic disciplines of the Spirit are activities such as prayer, study, fasting, solitude, silence, work, worship, celebration, fellowship, submission, confession, service, and so forth. These are the spirituality-forming behaviors Jesus himself practiced, personally taught his original disciples to employ, and, through the Holy Spirit, has inspired his followers living in later eras to observe.

In fact, it's due to the inspiring work of the Spirit that a large body of literary works exists to help readers—ordinary Christians like you and me—to master the spiritual disciplines. A cursory survey of these classic works on Christian spirituality reveals the experience of many sincere Christ-followers over the span of two millennia: by engaging in these spiritual disciplines, we put ourselves in a position where the Holy Spirit can form the character of Christ within us—so that we, filled with the supernatural power of God's eternal kingdom, can begin living a "Colossians 3 kind of life." It's upon these devotional classics (as well as Scripture) that Willard grounds his thinking about the nature and importance of the disciplines and toward which he focuses the attention of his students.[4]

My Own Spiritual Renaissance

While I don't claim to be an expert on spiritual formation, I do know something about one thing: my own spiritual journey. Several years ago, in a doctor of ministry seminar entitled "Spirituality and Ministry," I was privileged to sit under the tutelage of Dallas Willard. This postgraduate educational experience proved to be genuinely life changing. This was true not only because of Willard's teaching but also because participation in the seminar required me to read at least four thousand pages—*before* the two-week intensive seminar—from that body of classic literary works devoted to the theme of Christian spirituality. The bottom line is that weeks before this course actually commenced, this pre-seminar reading assignment had already begun to affect me in a deep, transformational manner.

Before beginning this pre-seminar prep, I had been experiencing a gnawing and growing sense of powerlessness both in my pastoral ministry and in my personal life. Some words that coincided with my emotional state at that time would be *hurry, stress, anxiety, frustration, impatience,* and *melancholy.* As I began my reading regimen, my soul was in a very needy condition. Can you relate to this honest admission? Have you ever been in such a place? Are you there now?

Page after page, book after book—all devoted to the theme of Christian spirituality—I ran across passage after passage that seemed to address my impoverished spiritual state. Slowly but surely, a sense of hope grew inside me. Increasingly, I became convinced that it might someday be possible to become a person so filled with God that my life would exude love, peace, and joy instead of irritation, frustration, drivenness, and despair. I began to picture myself as a truly Christlike person with a new ability to pray prayers that make a difference in people's lives; a new capacity to resist the tyranny of lust; a new freedom not to care so much about what others think of me; a new power in my preaching and teaching ministries; a new effectiveness in sharing Christ with those outside the community of faith; and a new confidence in the fact that, when this life ends, I will find myself in the arms of a gracious, merciful, life-giving Jesus. Again I ask, who wouldn't want this?

To be more specific, as I was fulfilling this pre-seminar reading assignment, I began to notice a particular theme recurring in the books I studied. At the heart of many of the approaches to Christian spirituality that have been offered over the years is the idea that it's possible to learn to live moment by moment in the felt presence of the resurrected and ascended Jesus. It's possible to approach all the events in the course of a day with a sense that we're not alone: that Christ is right there with us, loving us, encouraging us, enabling us to respond to this or that situation or person the way he would. Thus, in addition to everything else I learned from reading dozens of these classic texts on Christian spirituality, *I was exposed to the life-altering concept of Christ's empowering presence.*

This concept was reinforced by Willard's teaching to such an extent that, by the time the two-week seminar was over, I had become absolutely convinced that it is Christ's empowering presence that enables the sincere Christ-follower to live a "Colossians 3 kind of life": putting to death whatever belongs to our carnal, earthly nature (Colossians 3:5–11) and putting on the "new self" that is capable of living life in a refreshing, enjoyable, God-pleasing manner

(Colossians 3:12–17). In short, I came to believe that *the daily pursuit of Christ's empowering presence (which I will sometimes refer to simply as "the pursuit") is at the very heart of Christian spirituality.*

Again, who wouldn't want this? Who wouldn't want to experience the spiritual transformation described by Paul in Colossians 3:5–17? Who wouldn't want to move through the day a little less inclined toward impatience, hurry, worry, insecurity, resentment, envy, gossip, anger, and lust? Who wouldn't want to spend more time each day loving and serving others and trusting and praising God? Honestly, wouldn't it be wonderful—truly wonderful—to be able to live a different way?

The Way Forward

Assuming the *Newsweek* article cited earlier is accurate—that our world really is filled with "hungry people, looking for a deeper relationship with God"—I've written this book with the aim of helping people learn to experience the empowering presence of Christ. From the outset, my goal has been to produce a rich, devotional resource for your daily walk with Christ. I'd like to think that in the days, weeks, months, and years ahead you will be able (and inclined) to pick up this volume and find a powerful quote, from either the Scriptures or a Christian devotional classic, that reinspires you to keep at the pursuit of Christ's empowering presence. And yet my intention is that this volume be much more than just a compendium of inspiring quotes. Hopefully my commentary on these quotes, as well as what I have to say about my own spiritual journey, will also be of assistance.

Let's look ahead, now, at the way this book is organized. In his work *Renovation of the Heart,* Dallas Willard argues that there is a general pattern to all human accomplishment, including spiritual formation. He uses the acrostic "VIM" to help his readers keep this general pattern in mind. The letters in this acrostic represent Vision,

Intention, and Means. Willard explains: "If we are to be spiritually formed in Christ, we must have and must implement the appropriate *vision, intention,* and *means.* Not just any path we take will do. If this VIM pattern is not put in place properly and held there, Christ simply will not be formed in us."[5]

Though Willard intends this pattern to refer to the process of spiritual formation as a whole, I want to make use of it as an organizing framework for our discussion of the pursuit of Christ's empowering presence in particular. Thus, in part one of this work, I attempt to cast a clear *vision* of what the experience of Christ's empowering presence looks like. Willard speaks of the great need for Christians to "master the masters" as we attempt to live a Christ-focused life.[6] With this goal in mind, three chapters provide a historical survey of the way in which this important spiritual endeavor has been described in the writings of Brother Lawrence (chapter 1); the earliest Christians, the Desert Fathers, Saint Francis of Assisi, Thomas à Kempis, Ignatius of Loyola, Francis de Sales, and Jeremy Taylor (chapter 2); and some contemporary spiritual life authors such as Frank Laubach, A. W. Tozer, Leslie Weatherhead, Dallas Willard, Jan Johnson, Richard Foster, and John Ortberg (chapter 3). These chapters give not a dry history, but a rich, inspiring treatment of the prominent role the pursuit of Christ's empowering presence has played, and is playing, in the history of Christian spirituality.

The goal of part two of this work is to help readers form for themselves a sturdy *intention* to make the experience of Christ's empowering presence a lifelong pursuit. Toward this end, I provide analyses of the biblical support for this spiritual practice from both the Old Testament (chapter 4) and the New Testament (chapter 5), along with a survey of many of the benefits of this practice as presented in the corpus of devotional literature (chapter 6). I hope to demonstrate that it makes good sense to become immediately engaged in "the pursuit." Not only does this approach to Christian spirituality possess biblical warrant, but also the benefits that accrue from it are just too valuable, too vital to our walk with Christ, to ignore. Thus, the three chapters that make up this section provide even more inspirational references to the pursuit of Christ's empowering presence.

In part three of *Christ's Empowering Presence,* I provide three discussions of the *means* by which this key spiritual dynamic can be experienced on a daily, moment-by-moment basis. In chapter 7, the focus is on a formal strategy for holy living put forward by the seventeenth-century Anglican churchman Jeremy Taylor—a strategy that centers on the practice of God's presence. Chapter 8 then offers specific suggestions for developing our own unique approach to engaging in "the pursuit." Gleaned from my perusal of thousands of pages of classic Christian texts, the numerous suggestions presented in this chapter are some of the most interesting and helpful pursuit-related prescriptions ever to have been put into print. Finally, in chapter 9, I describe briefly the manner in which I attempt to become and to remain centered in Christ in the course of a typical day. Again, I'd like to think that these three final chapters prove to be informative, motivational, and therefore wonderful resources for ongoing inspiration regarding "the pursuit."

In the conclusion of this book, I take advantage of one last opportunity to clarify what a successful engagement in "the pursuit" requires and to convince us that we really should do this: spend the rest of our lives improving our ability to live a "Colossians 3 kind of life" via Christ's empowering presence.

You Do Want This, Right?

Throughout this introductory chapter, I've posed these questions: Who wouldn't want this? Who wouldn't want to learn how to live a "Colossians 3 kind of life"? My assumption is that anyone bothering to pick up a book such as this (and read it this far) would.

And yet, I've been a pastor too long not to be aware that some churchgoing folks really don't want to experience genuine spiritual transformation. With his tongue planted firmly in his cheek, pastor and author Wilbur Rees skewers the spiritual complacency and consumerist mindset present in the hearts of many modern churchgoing people:

> I would like to buy $3 worth of God, please, not enough to explode my soul or disturb my sleep, but just enough to equal a cup of warm milk or a snooze in the sunshine. I don't want enough of Him to make me love a black man or pick beets with a migrant. I want ecstasy, not transformation; I want the warmth of the womb, not a new birth. I want a pound of the eternal in a paper sack. I would like to buy $3 worth of God, please.[7]

Judging by how often this satirical piece has appeared in the Christian blogosphere, it appears that many believers are concerned that its message indeed reflects a nominalism that is at work in the hearts of more than a few churchgoing Christians. If this is true, it's no wonder churches in Europe and North America have been less than effective at fulfilling Christ's call to function as salt and light in the midst of an increasingly post-Christian society (see Matthew 5:13–16).[8] *Could it be that too many churches are made up of congregants who have settled for a mere $3 worth of God?* How ironic that while many society members are spiritually hungry for an experience of God's presence, some church members are anything but!

So, how about you? Are you truly interested in living a life that is full of God, rather than settling for a mere $3 worth? Are you eager to discover how you might grow in your ability to actually forge a "Colossians 3 kind of life"?

I sincerely hope you make the decision to follow along, as I do my best to cast a clear *vision* of what the experience of Christ's empowering presence looks like, to inspire you to make it your personal *intention* to live the rest of your life enjoying Christ's empowering presence, and to provide you with the *means* by which this key spiritual dynamic can be experienced on a daily, moment-by-moment basis. While I can't claim to have completely mastered this activity in my own life, I've tasted of it enough to know that the phenomenon of Christ's empowering presence is real and that it possesses genuine transformational power. We really can do better at living a "Colossians 3 kind of life."

You know you want this! Right? Let's get started!

PART ONE

VISION:
WHAT THE PURSUIT
OF CHRIST'S EMPOWERING
PRESENCE LOOKS LIKE

BROTHER LAWRENCE:
A MOST POPULAR PRACTITIONER
OF "THE PURSUIT"

A ccording to Dallas Willard, engaging in fellowship with other followers of Christ, both ancient and contemporary, is a crucial practice in cultivating a healthy Christian spirituality.

> Some with whom we must have fellowship have long been dead, but they live on and are available to us through writings. Of course, many of these are in the Bible. Others are nearer to us in time, and some are our contemporaries. We need to devote much time to knowing them well. We must above all master the masters.[1]

There's a sense in which "mastering the masters" is what *Christ's Empowering Presence* is all about. Throughout this work we focus on what biblical authors and spiritual masters of the Christian tradition have said about the practice of "the pursuit." If my experience is any indication, then *fellowshipping* with these spiritual masters will prove to be nothing short of life changing.

We begin our journey toward a better understanding of Christ's empowering presence with an instructive and inspiring consideration of the example provided for us by a seventeenth-century French monk, who has come to be known as Brother Lawrence. This is our starting point not because Brother Lawrence was the first to practice "the pursuit," nor because his approach is somehow the best, but because the classic devotional work he inspired—*The Practice of the Presence of God*—is widely known among both Roman Catholic and Protestant believers.

Though we shouldn't feel the need to engage in this spiritual exercise in precisely the same manner as this godly monk, we dare not ignore what he had to say about it. How integral to Christian spirituality is "the pursuit"? How important is one's motive when engaging in this central spiritual discipline? How feasible is this approach to spiritual formation for people who lead extremely busy lives? In one way or another, Brother Lawrence addressed all of these issues.

A Brief Biography

Nicholas Herman (1610–1691) was born a peasant in Lorraine, France. During a stint in the army, Herman experienced a spiritual awakening as he gazed upon a barren, leafless tree in the dead of winter. In one sense, the desolate image apparently spoke to Herman of his current situation. Yet it also communicated to him a sense of hope, grounded in the knowledge that, come springtime, this same tree would once again come to life, bearing leaves, flowers, and fruit. Evidently, in this moment, an evangelical faith in the essential goodness, bigness, and dependability of God was born in his heart.

Sometime later, Herman suffered an injury to his sciatic nerve, forcing him to retire from the army as well as causing him chronic pain the rest of his life. After serving for a brief time as a valet to a Monsieur Fieuburt, Herman entered the Discalced (shoeless) Carmelite monastery in Paris as Brother Lawrence of the Resurrection.[2]

Within the monastery, Brother Lawrence was assigned to work in the kitchen, where he labored for fifteen years. Though he possessed a natural aversion to this type of work, it was in that busy, noisy kitchen that he learned to commune continually with God and to perform every mundane chore as an act of worship.

We know of the life and distinctive spirituality of Brother Lawrence chiefly through *The Practice of the Presence of God*, which is essentially made up of several conversations and letters he exchanged with Monsieur Joseph de Beaufort, chief envoy of the Archbishop of Paris. After Brother Lawrence's death, his fellow monks found among his things two writings, now known as *Gathered Thoughts* and *Spiritual Maxims*. These documents present even more counsel in how to attain the presence of God, along with the benefits of doing so. Yet another resource is a diminutive document entitled *The Character of Brother Lawrence* (also known as *The Life of Brother Lawrence*)—a brief sketch of Brother Lawrence as he appeared to those who knew him best, probably authored by Monsieur de Beaufort, the chronicler of the conversations and letters.[3]

It is to these four concise but profound documents that we turn in order to form a foundational understanding of what it means to pursue Christ's empowering presence. I will cite excerpts from two different versions of these four works. One rendition retains a beautiful though antiquated English translation; the other is an updated English edition in which words, expressions, and sentence structure have been revised to make the material more accessible to the modern reader. I have pressed the quaint version into service only when pertinent sections could not be located in the updated account or when the more traditional rendering communicates some important sense of meaning that doesn't show up in the revised edition.

I sincerely hope that, when reading the antiquated material presented here, no one feels thrown into the deep end of the pool. On the other hand, we do have to start somewhere. So let's take a deep breath and dive right in!

The Essence of Christ's Empowering Presence

According to Brother Lawrence, it's both possible and desirable to develop the life habit of *continually conversing with God.* Monsieur de Beaufort writes:

> Brother Lawrence insisted that, to be constantly aware of God's presence, it is necessary to form the habit of continually talking with Him throughout each day. To think that we must abandon conversation with Him in order to deal with the world is erroneous. Instead, as we nourish our souls by seeing God in His exaltation, we will derive great joy at being His.[4]

Thus the pursuit of Christ's empowering presence, in the simplest sense, involves our learning how to maintain with Jesus an *ongoing internal conversation,* regardless of whatever else is going on around us. In de Beaufort's account of his several interactions with Brother Lawrence, we find the following passage in which the godly monk elaborates on the nature of such an ongoing conversation:

> Today Brother Lawrence spoke to me quite openly and with great enthusiasm about his manner of going to God. He said the most important part resides in renouncing, once and for all, whatever does not lead to God. This allows us to become involved in a continuous conversation with Him in a simple and unhindered manner.
>
> All we have to do is to recognize God as being intimately present within us. Then we may speak directly to Him every time we need to ask for help, to know His will in moments

of uncertainty, and to do whatever He wants us to do in a way that pleases Him. We should offer our work to Him before we begin and thank Him afterward for the privilege of having done it for His sake. This continuous conversation should also include praising and loving God incessantly for His infinite goodness and perfection.[5]

Another glimpse into Brother Lawrence's approach to spirituality comes in his own words, as recorded by de Beaufort. The first thing we learn from the good brother's sharing is that, rather than engaging in all sorts of elaborate devotional rituals during his formal prayer times, his habit was simply to meditate on the attributes of God and Christ.

> When I first entered the monastery, I looked upon God as the beginning and the end of all my thoughts and all the feelings of my soul. During the hours that were designated for prayer, I meditated on the truth and character of God that we must accept by the light of faith, rather than spending time in laborious meditations and readings. By meditating on Jesus Himself, I advanced in my knowledge of this lovable Person with whom I resolved to dwell always.[6]

Brother Lawrence goes on to explain how his custom was to take this sense of Christ's presence with him into the rest of his day:

> Completely immersed in my understanding of God's majesty, I used to shut myself up in the kitchen. Alone, after having done everything that was necessary for my work, I devoted myself to prayer in the time that was left.
>
> The prayer time was really taken at both the beginning and the end of my work. At the beginning of my duties, I would say to the Lord with confidence, "My God, since You are with me and since, by Your will, I must occupy myself with external things, please grant me the grace to remain with You, in Your presence. Work with me, so that my work might

be the very best. Receive as an offering of love both my work and all my affections."

During my work, I would always continue to speak to the Lord as though He were right with me, offering Him my services and thanking Him for His assistance. Also, at the end of my work, I used to examine it carefully. If I found good in it, I thanked God. If I noticed faults, I asked His forgiveness without being discouraged, and then went on with my work, still dwelling in Him.

Thus, continuing in the practice of conversing with God throughout each day and quickly seeking His forgiveness when I fell or strayed, His presence has become as easy and natural to me now as it once was difficult to attain.[7]

These foundation-forming passages are crucial to adequately understand what it meant for Brother Lawrence to practice the presence of God, as well as what it might mean for us to engage in the pursuit of Christ's empowering presence. Among other things, these readings suggest that such an approach to Christian spirituality might involve our learning to

- begin each day doing our best to prayerfully recognize and appreciate God's ongoing, intimate presence with us;
- address ourselves to God every waking moment throughout the day, continually calling on him for wisdom, discernment, and grace (empowerment) to do his will;
- offer absolutely everything we do as a gift to God *before* we act;
- pause inwardly to give thanks to God for his empowering assistance *after* we've performed each action as unto him;
- continually praise, adore, and love God even as we go about our daily business;
- periodically evaluate how well we've remained mindful of God's presence;

- trust in God's forgiveness when our attempts at practicing his presence have been less than satisfactory, forgiving ourselves, and pressing on with the resolve to do better in the future.

Reflect carefully upon this list of activities. As we go forward in our study, we will discover that these are the most basic themes upon which nearly all discussions of Christ's empowering presence focus. These, however, are not the only passages in *The Practice of the Presence of God* that provide helpful depictions of this holy habit. This small book is filled with passages that are both informative and inspiring. I'm intrigued, in particular, by (a) the number of passages in which Brother Lawrence insists that the key motive for practicing God's presence is an attitude of love (rather than of fear), (b) those passages in which Brother Lawrence indicates that his engagement in this one practice constituted the main means by which he cultivated his spirituality, and (c) those passages that insist this central spiritual discipline can be engaged in despite a very busy lifestyle.

Since these three issues seem to be at the heart of Brother Lawrence's approach to spirituality, let's take a look at them one by one.

Love: The Only Motive

Reading through *The Practice of the Presence of God,* one cannot help but notice Brother Lawrence's insistence that the ultimate and only motive for this spiritual discipline must be a sincere desire to commune with and serve a good God. Implied is Brother Lawrence's concern that someone might succumb to the temptation to turn the pursuit of Christ's empowering presence into a fear-based religious work or to engage in it merely to impress his or her peers. It's easy to see how this could happen in a religious community such as that housed in a monastery. But I think it's possible for us noncloistered followers of Christ to be tempted in these ways as well. Sometimes it's easy to allow our embrace of grace to falter or to care a bit too much about appearing spiritual before our family and friends. These kinds of concerns best explain the following passages drawn from the records of Brother Lawrence's conversations and letters—passages that in one way or another refer to the godly monk's love for the Lord. In reference to his observations of Brother Lawrence, de Beaufort writes:

> Brother Lawrence confided to me that the foundation of his spiritual life was the faith that revealed to him the exalted position of God. Once this became secure in the depths of his heart, he was easily able to do all his actions for the love of God.[8]

> Our brother remarked that some people go only as far as their regular devotions, stopping there and neglecting love, which is the purpose of those devotions.[9] This could easily be seen in their actions and explained why they possessed so little solid virtue.
>
> Neither skill nor knowledge is needed to go to God, he added. All that is necessary is a heart dedicated entirely and solely to Him out of love for Him above all others.[10]

> The most effective way Brother Lawrence had for communicating with God was to simply do his ordinary work. He did this obediently, out of a pure love for God.[11]

The next two excerpts are presented in the first person, coming from Brother Lawrence himself. They too emphasize the good brother's motive of love.

> There is no sweeter manner of living in the world than continuous communion with God. Only those who have experienced it can understand. However, I don't advise you to practice it for the sole purpose of gaining consolation for

your problems. Seek it, rather, because God wills it and out of love for Him.[12]

> I feel unable to express what is going on inside me right now. I'm not anxious about my purpose in life because I only want to do God's will. I wouldn't even lift a straw from the ground against His order or for any other motive than love for Him. Pure love of Him is all that keeps me going.[13]

According to Proverbs 16:2, our motives matter to God. I trust that from this section you recognize how important it was to Brother Lawrence that the practice of the presence of God be engaged in with the right motive. We must not turn this holy habit into a legalistic attempt to mollify the wrath of an angry God. Neither should we pursue this practice in an attempt to have our peers notice our superlative piety. In a word, the only appropriate motive for pursuing Christ's empowering presence is *love*—our love for him and a quiet confidence in his love for us.

The Heart of Christian Spirituality

Another dominant theme runs throughout our resources for understanding the thought and practice of Brother Lawrence: practicing God's presence is at the very heart of Christian spirituality. Indeed, there are places in these writings where Brother Lawrence seems to suggest that this one spiritual discipline is all that's necessary for the sincere Christ-follower to grow in his or her walk with God! For example, Brother Lawrence said, according to de Beaufort, "he was more united to God in his outward employments than when he left them for devotion and retirement."[14] At the very least, this brief statement implies that the godly monk's private devotional practices offered him no more of a sense of intimacy with God than when he was engaged in more mundane matters.

This same idea finds expression in another passage, in which de Beaufort records Brother Lawrence insisting that our sanctification depends not so much on our engaging in special spiritual exercises, but simply on making sure that what we normally do each day is performed for God's sake rather than for our own. The good brother goes on to critique those Christians who mistake the means for the end—that is, literally becoming addicted to the performance of "certain works," convinced they are serving God when, in reality, they are really serving themselves![15]

By "certain works," Brother Lawrence seemed to have in mind the idea of special devotional activities. This is indicated by the fact that, in yet another place, Monsieur de Beaufort describes Brother Lawrence as follows:

> He believed it was a serious mistake to think of our prayer time as being different from any other. Our actions should unite us with God when we are involved in our daily activities, just as our prayers unite us with Him in our quiet devotions.
>
> He said his prayers consisted totally and simply of God's presence. His soul was resting in God, having lost its awareness of everything but love of Him. When he wasn't in prayer, he felt practically the same way. Remaining near to God, he praised and blessed Him with all his strength. Because of this, his life was full of continual joy.[16]

This is actually one of several passages where Brother Lawrence seems to suggest that practicing the presence of God was, for him, the main manner in which he cultivated his spirituality. Another example of this type of passage is located in *Spiritual Maxims*. In that work, written by Brother Lawrence's own hand, we find this bold statement: "The most holy and necessary practice in our spiritual life is the presence of God."[17]

In some passages we almost hear Brother Lawrence say that the only reason he would engage in any other form of spiritual devotion was if the order to which he belonged mandated it. For example, in one of his letters to de Beaufort, Brother Lawrence confesses:

> I have given up all but my intercessory prayers to focus my attention on remaining in His holy presence. I keep my attention on God in a simple, loving way. This is my soul's secret experience of the actual, unceasing presence of God. It gives me such contentment and joy that I sometimes feel compelled to do rather childish things to control it.[18]

Similarly, in *The Character (or Life) of Brother Lawrence,* de Beaufort includes a descriptive paragraph suggesting that, since Brother Lawrence's activities—both secular as well as those traditionally considered more sacred—involved his pursuit of Christ's empowering presence, his spiritual mentor saw no real difference between them. Monsieur de Beaufort writes:

> Everything was the same to him—every place, every job. The good brother found God everywhere, as much while he was repairing shoes as while he was praying with the community. He was in no hurry to go on retreats because he found the same God to love and adore in his ordinary work as in the depth of the desert.[19]

It should be apparent to us by now that Brother Lawrence held a high view of the practice of God's presence as the very center of Christian spirituality. His engagement in "the pursuit" was at the very heart of his approach to spiritual formation. Thus, it's fitting to conclude this section with one final quote: "Brother Lawrence called the practice of the presence of God the easiest and shortest way to attain Christian perfection and to be protected from sin."[20]

Anytime, Anywhere!

Finally, a third important theme in Brother Lawrence's thinking about spirituality is that a person's busyness is no excuse for failing to practice the presence of God! Passages scattered throughout our resource materials insist that it's possible to maintain a vibrant inner sense of God's loving, empowering presence, regardless of the many outward activities our busy lives might entail. In his description, de Beaufort recounts that Brother Lawrence once told him the following:

> For me the time of action does not differ from the time of prayer, and in the noise and clatter of my kitchen, while several persons are together calling for as many different things, I possess God in as great tranquility as when upon my knees at the Blessed Sacrament.[21]

Brother Lawrence's biographer goes on to provide the world with this famous passage:

> I am giving you a picture of a lay brother serving in a kitchen; let me then use his own words: "We can do *little* things for GOD; I turn the cake that is frying on the pan for the love of Him, and that done, if there is nothing else to call me, I prostrate myself in worship before Him, Who has given me grace to work; afterwards I rise happier than a king. It is enough for me to pick but a straw from the ground for the love of GOD."[22]

What effect did integrating spirituality with his daily work have upon Brother Lawrence? Though later in this book we explore the benefits of a daily pursuit of Christ's empowering presence, it's appropriate here to include a passage describing the impact practicing the presence of God had upon this particularly popular practitioner. Rounding off his record of the four conversations he had with Brother Lawrence, de Beaufort offers these concluding remarks:

> As Brother Lawrence had found such an advantage in walking in the presence of God, it was natural for him to recommend it earnestly to others; but his example was a stronger inducement than any arguments he could propose.

> His very countenance was edifying, such a sweet and calm devotion appearing in it as could not but affect the beholders. And it was observed that in the greatest hurry of business in the kitchen he still preserved his recollection and heavenly-mindedness. He was never hasty nor loitering, but did each thing in its season, with an even, uninterrupted composure and tranquility of spirit.[23]

Evidently it *is* possible to pursue Christ's empowering presence despite a busy lifestyle! Possessing a plate full of mundane responsibilities is no excuse for neglecting "the pursuit." The example of Brother Lawrence establishes this theme as well as any spiritual master I can think of.

The overarching goal of this chapter is to introduce the concept of Christ's empowering presence by carefully considering the life and work of one of its most famous practitioners: Brother Lawrence of the Resurrection. During the process, I've cited a number of passages from the resource materials that never fail to reinspire me in my own practice of the presence of God. Rather than feeling as if you've been thrown into the deep end of the pool, I hope you will consider Brother Lawrence's advocacy of "the pursuit" to be a life vest that can save you from "drowning" in the spiritually deadening demands of daily living. With that thought in mind, I conclude this chapter with a quote drawn from Brother Lawrence's ninth letter to Monsieur de Beaufort:

> We cannot avoid the dangers of life without God's continual help, so we should ask Him for it ceaselessly. But how can we ask for help unless we are with Him? To be with Him, we must cultivate the holy habit of thinking of Him often.
>
> You will tell me that I always say the same thing. What can I say? It is true. I don't know an easier method, nor do I practice any other, so I advise this one to everybody. We have to know someone before we truly love him. In order to

know God, we must think about Him often. Once we get to know Him, we will think about Him even more often, because where our treasure is, there also is our heart![24]

To be sure, we would all do well to consider carefully the wise counsel offered by this saintly man of God. And yet, as valuable as Brother Lawrence is to our understanding of Christ's empowering presence, it would be wrong to think that his was the first and last word on this topic. Other folks in the history of spirituality have also advocated the practice of the presence of God, though the exercise has not always been referred to in just that way. In the next couple of chapters, we will survey what other spiritual masters have said about the pursuit of Christ's empowering presence. In other words, our "fellowship" with the spiritual masters has only just begun!

—————— 2 ——————

SOME ANCIENT SPIRITUAL MASTERS FAMILIAR WITH "THE PURSUIT"

I n their best-selling book *The Sacred Romance: Drawing Closer to the Heart of God,* John Eldredge and the late Brent Curtis suggest that, in the lives of too many contemporary Christians, something important is missing in their approach to spirituality.

> For centuries prior to our Modern Era, the church viewed the gospel as a Romance, a cosmic drama whose themes permeated our own stories and drew together all the random scenes in a redemptive wholeness. But our rationalistic approach to life, which has dominated Western culture for hundreds of years, has stripped us of that, leaving a faith that is barely more than mere fact-telling. Modern evangelicalism reads like an IRS 1040 form: It's true, all the data is there, but it doesn't take your breath away. As British theologian Alister McGrath warns, the Bible is not primarily a doctrinal sourcebook: "To reduce revelation to principles or concepts is to

suppress the element of mystery, holiness and wonder to God's self-disclosure. 'First principles' may enlighten and inform; they do not force us to our knees in reverence and awe, as with Moses at the burning bush, or the disciples in the presence of the risen Christ."[1]

This provocative quote distinguishes between premodern spirituality, which was oriented around the theme of a sacred romance, and modern spirituality (if we can call it that), which is hyperrational and scholastic in nature. The problem with the latter, say these authors, is that it "doesn't take your breath away" (Eldredge and Curtis), and it isn't sufficient to "force us to our knees in reverence and awe" (McGrath).

In the introduction to this book, I suggested that at the heart of a healthy Christian spirituality is an exercise that involves doing our best to maintain a perpetual sense of conversational communion with the risen Christ. The goal of this chapter (and the one that follows) is to provide a chronologically ordered survey of the manner in which some of Christianity's greatest spiritual masters, from the earliest era to the present, have alluded to and advocated for a Christ-revering, awe-inspiring approach to spirituality. Though the various versions of "the pursuit" surveyed in these two chapters may differ in small ways, all of them seem to focus on the same goal: an intimate, interactive relationship with Christ that produces within us not only a profound sense of reverence and awe but also the capacity for a "Colossians 3 kind of life."

The Earliest Christians

The first followers of Christ had their hands full turning the world upside down (see some translations of Acts 17:6) and laying the foundation for the church (see Ephesians 2:19–20). And, they were forced to tackle both of these tasks while also dealing with persecution from without and heresies from within. There's a real sense in which the main aim of the earliest Christians was to define, defend, and spread the true faith, while doing their best to avoid being killed on account of it! It shouldn't surprise us, then, to discover that most of the writings from this formative era tend not to be deep, extensive reflections on the nature of Christian spirituality. Still, there is good reason to believe that the spirituality practiced by the earliest disciples of Jesus involved an ongoing experience of his resurrection reality.

The pursuit of Christ's empowering presence is reflected in the writings of the New Testament (surveyed in chapter 5). This fact alone should convince us that believers living in the first few decades of the Christian era were familiar with this particular spiritual discipline. Richard J. Woods, in his book *Christian Spirituality: God's Presence through the Ages,* also supports the idea that members of the early church endeavored to practice the presence of God. He insists, "from the beginning, Christian spirituality as a whole always focused on awareness of and faith in the abiding presence of God. . . . In fact, Christian spirituality originated and developed as a growing consciousness of the special reality of God's presence as companion and friend in Jesus and his first disciples."[2]

If Woods' assessment is correct, then the spirituality of the earliest Christians centered on an awareness of God's presence in their lives, just as Jesus himself had experienced the divine presence. Thus, to understand fully the spirituality of the earliest Christians, we must first understand the spirituality of Jesus, which, in turn, requires a basic understanding of the spirituality at work in the historic Jewish community out of which the Messiah emerged.

The Spirituality of the Old Testament Saints

The spirituality that earmarked the Jewish community in the Old Testament era, Woods maintains, was steeped in a sense of

God's manifest presence. Even in the days when the old covenant held sway, the people of God were enlivened by the possibility of an intimate communion with him.[3] Describing the spirituality at work in the Old Testament community of faith, Woods highlights the way in which the Scriptures refer to biblical characters experiencing God's real presence in an intimate, interactive manner.

> The great heroes of Israel's history were men and women who knew God in the intimacy of elect companionship, such as Abraham and Sarah, who entertained Divinity under the oaks of Mamre, or Jacob and Joseph, who heard voices in the night and dreamed strange dreams. Moses conversed with Omnipotence face to face and even glimpsed the backside of God's glory. Judges like Deborah, Jael, and Gideon haggled and argued with God like fishwives. Samuel and Elijah heard the whisper of Infinity in the utter silence of the midnight desert. David loved his Lord passionately, singing and dancing and making music on the harp for his Divine Friend. The great prophets and champions were pursued and penetrated by the ardor of that Lover—Amos, Hosea, Isaiah, Jeremiah, Judith, Esther, and the Maccabees. Therefore, when Israel wished to remember God, she also recalled God's friends, those who had *known* God in the immediacy of present experience, an intimacy ultimately meant for all.[4]

Does it surprise you to find someone describing the spirituality of the Old Testament saints in this way? Woods has done the Christian community a tremendous service by reminding us of how important the experience of God's empowering presence was to the Jewish spirituality, which apparently affected Jesus and his first followers profoundly.

Jesus' Spirituality

While acknowledging that we lack an exhaustive understanding of all that went on in Jesus' interior life, Woods suggests that the testimony provided by the Gospels is sufficient to conclude that the heart of Jesus' spirituality was a "tender and intimate relationship with God, whom Jesus addressed in prayer and exhortation as 'Father,' sometimes in the familiar Aramaic form *Abba*."[5]

Woods goes on to explain that even though the idea of the fatherhood of God was not absent from Jewish spirituality, still "Jesus added a dimension of proximity and awareness that struck his contemporaries as novel and even unsettling."[6] In other words, while it wasn't unheard of for Jewish rabbis to speak of Yahweh as a father, they certainly didn't do so the way Jesus did. In fact, with such an intimate, interactive relationship with God, Jesus asserted before his disciples and detractors that everything he did was at the behest of his Father (see John 14:10; 14:31)—that is, he did only the things he saw his Father doing (see John 5:19; 10:37), and he said only the things he heard his Father saying (see John 5:30; 8:28; 12:49; 14:24; 15:15). These are bold allusions to the intimacy Jesus experienced with God!

The Spirituality of Jesus' Followers

Not only was Jesus' spirituality earmarked by a sense of interactive intimacy with God, but the Gospels portray him encouraging his disciples to likewise begin conceiving of God as a loving, heavenly Abba, with whom they too could experience profound intimacy (for example, see Matthew 6).[7]

Going further, while both Christians and Jews living in the first century might have embraced the idea of experiencing God's presence, the thing that set early Christian spirituality apart from its Jewish counterpart was that Jesus went on to lay claim to his own divinity. According to Jesus, to know him was to know God (see John 8:19; 14:7), to see him was to see God (see John 12:45; 14:9), to receive him was to receive God (see Mark 9:37), to hate him was to hate God (see John 15:23), and to honor him was to honor God (see John 5:23). Thus, despite their common focus on the experience of the presence of God, there's a big difference between the spirituality of Jews and Christians. Woods describes this huge difference as "the meaning and person of Jesus, especially the central matter of God's unique presence in Jesus."[8]

The Gospels also portray Jesus making some important promises to his disciples regarding his commitment to be *with* them no matter when, or where, or what. For example, in Matthew 18, Jesus encourages his disciples to expect a helpful sense of his presence whenever two or three of them gather in his name (Matthew 18:20). And in the last few verses of Matthew, Jesus promises his first followers that he will be with them always, even to the end of the age (Matthew 28:20).

So, the earliest Christians possessed not only the notion of an intimate, interactive relationship with God but also the conviction that such a relationship could be experienced through the person of Jesus, who promised to somehow be *with* his disciples even after his death, resurrection, and ascension. Thus, the foundation was laid for a spirituality that would involve the pursuit of Christ's empowering presence.

Is there any indication that the earliest followers of Jesus practiced such a spirituality? I believe there is. One unique feature of the first three hundred years of the Christian era was that many chose to suffer martyrdom rather than deny their relationship with Christ. Though space will not permit it, a thorough analysis of the speeches and letters of these martyrs might indicate the nature of the spirituality that fueled their commitment in the face of great suffering. In the New Testament, we find the record of the church's very first martyr, Stephen. The account indicates how Stephen, as he died, experienced the empowering presence of Christ in a powerful (perhaps even paradigmatic) manner (see Acts 7:54–60). If this record of the church's first martyr is any indication of the expectancy possessed by other believers during that primitive era, then we may be justified in concluding that the spirituality of many of the earliest Christians did focus on the experience of the empowering presence of Christ!

The Desert Fathers

Church historians tell us that once the Christian faith became legalized in AD 313 and then made the official religion of the Roman Empire in AD 380, the moral and spiritual tone of the church became lax. Instead of paying a price for owning the Christian faith, identifying oneself as a Christian became the fashionable, politically expedient thing to do. As the church swelled with adherents whose faith was nominal at best, its spiritual purity diminished. Convinced that the institutional church had become irrevocably worldly, many zealous Christ-followers fled to the Egyptian wilderness, where they sought to kindle afresh a spirituality that enabled an experience of intimacy with a holy God.

Richard Woods explains that the first Christian hermits desired to find a remote place for prayer and fasting as well as "to be alone with God."[9] Thus, there's a real sense in which the monastic movement was born out of a desire to experience Christ's empowering presence. It's true that the Desert Fathers—the founders of the Christian monastic movement—didn't speak of "practicing the presence of God" as such. However, it's apparent that the concept and experience of Christ's empowering presence was very familiar to them.

One way of making this connection is to consider the devotional writings of the late Henri Nouwen, a Roman Catholic priest and professor of pastoral theology and psychology. Nouwen held positions in several prestigious universities before responding to the call to imitate the downward mobility and servant-heart of Jesus. After briefly serving as a missionary to the poor in Latin America and lecturing stateside on those experiences, Nouwen devoted the remainder of his life to caring for the mentally handicapped. Roman Catholics and Protestants alike revere his writings on Christian spirituality.

In one of his best-known books, *The Way of the Heart,* Nouwen offers a treatment of the spirituality of the desert fathers and mothers. In the process, he focuses on the practice of solitude and repeatedly references the goal of "encounter" with God and Christ. Nouwen indicates, for example, that the purpose of solitude is that we might struggle with ourselves and be encountered by God. "Solitude is the place of the great struggle and the great encounter—the struggle against the compulsions of the false self, and the encounter with the loving God who offers himself as the substance of the new self."[10]

Elsewhere, Nouwen is careful to specify that the primary task in solitude is to seek an encounter with Christ. "We enter into solitude first of all to meet our Lord and to be with him and him alone. Our primary task in solitude, therefore, is not to pay undue attention to the many faces which assail us, but to keep the eyes of our mind and heart on him who is our divine savior."[11]

Nouwen goes on to offer the following rationale for a daily experience of solitude that leads to an empowering encounter with Christ:

> Precisely because our secular milieu offers us so few spiritual disciplines, we have to develop our own. We have, indeed, to fashion our own desert where we can withdraw every day, shake off our compulsions, and dwell in the gentle healing presence of our Lord. Without such a desert we will lose our own soul while preaching the gospel to others. But with such a spiritual abode, we will become increasingly conformed to him in whose Name we minister.[12]

As you can see, Nouwen speaks of our need to "fashion our own desert," where we can daily "dwell in the gentle healing presence of our Lord." This certainly suggests that he is doing more than just affirming the value of a periodic retreat to some remote location. No, his counsel calls for us to learn to practice solitude every day!

This quote from the writings of Henri Nouwen makes it clear that he conceived of this discipline not as an end in itself, but as a means of experiencing Christ's empowering presence:

> Although the discipline of solitude asks us to set aside time and space, what finally matters is that our hearts become like quiet cells where God can dwell, wherever we go and whatever we do. The more we train ourselves to spend time with God and him alone, the more we will discover that God is with us at all times and in all places. Then we will be able to recognize him even in the midst of a busy and active life. Once the solitude of time and space has become a solitude of the heart, we will never have to leave that solitude. We will be able to live in the spiritual life in any place and any time. Thus the discipline of solitude enables us to live active lives in the world, while remaining always in the presence of the living God.[13]

Sounds a lot like Brother Lawrence, doesn't it? To the degree that Nouwen's emphasis upon solitude is in touch with the impetus that drove the original desert fathers into the wilderness, we can safely assume that the pursuit of Christ's empowering presence was at least part of what their spirituality was about.

Saint Francis of Assisi

What do you think of when you hear the name Saint Francis of Assisi? Does your mind immediately picture an Italian youth rejecting his father's wealth, including even the clothing he had received from his father? How about a brown-robed monk repairing a dilapidated church or begging his daily bread? What of the itinerant preacher who is said to have preached not only to large crowds of human beings but, on a few occasions, to members of the animal kingdom as well?

Depending on your knowledge of church history, you may already be aware of these interesting details of Saint Francis' life (1181/1182–1226). But even the well-versed historian might not know that the passion of Saint Francis' soul was to pursue the empowering presence of Christ. How do we know this to be true? In his biography of Saint Francis, Bonaventure poetically describes his hero, alluding several times to Francis' engagement in "the pursuit":

> Who can describe
> the fervent charity
> which burned within Francis, the *friend of the Bridegroom?*
> Like a glowing coal,
> he seemed totally absorbed
> in the flame of divine love.
> Whenever he heard of the love of God,
> he was at once excited, moved and inflamed
> as if an inner chord of his heart
> had been plucked by the plectrum
> of the external voice.
> He used to say
> that to offer the love of God in exchange for an alms
> was a noble prodigality
> and that those who valued it less than money
> were most foolish,
> because the incalculable of divine love alone
> was sufficient to purchase
> the kingdom of heaven.
> And he used to say
> that greatly should the love be loved

of him who loved us so greatly.
Aroused by all things to the love of God,
he rejoiced in all the works of the Lord's hands
and from these joy-producing manifestations
he rose to their life-giving
principle and cause.
In beautiful things
he saw Beauty itself
and through his *vestiges* imprinted on creation
he followed his Beloved everywhere,
making from all things a ladder
by which he could climb up
and embrace him who is utterly desirable.[14]

Bonaventure followed this lovely set of verses with a more prosaic, but no less informative description of the famous monk's commitment to Christ. Please notice in the following excerpt how the pursuit of Christ's empowering presence led Francis to a radical engagement in classic disciplines of the Spirit, such as solitude, fasting, prayer, and worship. Notice also the effect this special season of seeking had upon him. Bonaventure writes:

> Jesus Christ crucified always rested like a bundle of myrrh in the bosom of Francis' soul (Cant. 1:12), and he longed to be totally transformed into him by the fire of ecstatic love. As a sign of his special devotion to him, Francis spent time from the feast of Epiphany through forty successive days—that period when Christ was hidden in the desert—secluded in a lonely place, shut up in a cell, with as little food and drink as possible, fasting, praying and praising God without interruption. He was drawn to Christ with such fervent love, and the Beloved (Cant. 1:12) returned such intimate love to him that God's servant always seemed to feel the presence of his

Savior before his eyes, as he once intimately revealed to his companions.[15]

Descriptions such as these lead us to believe that this thirteenth-century founder of the Franciscan order serves as another example of a spiritual master who experienced and advocated the empowering presence of Christ.

Thomas à Kempis

In the same way that *The Practice of the Presence of God* is familiar to many Protestant believers, I suspect the famous devotional work *The Imitation of Christ* is also. Though born in Germany, Thomas à Kempis (1380–1471) spent most of his adult life in the monastery of Mount St. Agnes, located near Zwolle, Holland. He functioned there as a priest, monk, Scripture copyist, and author in his own right. Belonging to a religious community that emphasized practical love for one another and union with God (the Brothers of Common Life), Thomas' spirituality led him to focus on the idea of pursuing an intimate, faithful friendship with Christ. The promise of having Jesus as a dear friend with whom one can maintain a real relationship is a prevalent theme in Thomas' magnum opus, *The Imitation of Christ*. The key to cultivating a vibrant Christian spirituality, says Thomas, is our focus. Will we focus our attention each day on everything but Jesus, or will we give him space in our lives?

In the process of encouraging a proper focus, Thomas could exhort his readers to pursue intimacy with Christ using arguments that were both positive and negative in tone. For example, admonishing his readers to recognize the vital importance of not ignoring Jesus in their daily lives, Thomas warns of the possibility of actually chasing away his presence.

> It is a great art to know how to hold converse with Jesus, and to know how to keep Jesus is wisdom indeed. Be humble

and a man of peace, and Jesus will abide with you. But if you turn aside to worldly things, you will soon cause Jesus to leave you, and you will lose His grace. And if you drive Him away and lose Him, with whom may you take refuge, and whom will you seek for your friend? Without a friend, you cannot live happily, and if Jesus is not your best friend, you will be exceedingly sad and lonely; so it is foolish to trust or delight in any other. It is better to have the whole world as your enemy than offend Jesus. Therefore, of all dear friends, let Jesus be loved first and above all.[16]

This is a somber warning indeed. And yet, in another place in *The Imitation of Christ,* Thomas takes a more encouraging tack, emphasizing the tremendous value of having Christ in our lives.

"The Kingdom of God is within you," says Our Lord. Turn to the Lord with all your heart, forsake this sorry world, and your soul shall find rest. Learn to turn from worldly things, and give yourself to spiritual things, and you will see the Kingdom of God come within you. For the Kingdom is peace and joy in the Holy Spirit; these are not granted to the wicked. Christ will come to you, and impart his consolations to you, if you prepare a worthy dwelling for Him in your hearts. All true glory and beauty is within, and there He delights to dwell. He often visits the spiritual man, and holds sweet discourse with him, granting him refreshing grace, great peace, and friendship exceeding all expectation.

Come then, faithful soul; prepare your heart for your Divine Spouse, that He might deign to come to you and dwell with you. For He says, "If any man love Me, he will keep My word; and We will come and make Our abode with him." Therefore welcome Christ, and deny entrance to all others. When you possess Christ, you are amply rich, and He will satisfy you. He will dispose and provide for you faithfully in everything, so that you need not rely on man. For men soon change and fail you; but Christ abides forever, and stands firmly by you to the end.[17]

Did you notice in this second, more encouraging passage that Thomas portrays Jesus not only as a great spiritual friend but also as a "Divine Spouse"? In the course of the journey we're taking together, we'll come across this imagery again. For now, the important thing is to allow our minds to contemplate how this "romance rhetoric" and "marital motif" adds a note of intimacy and increased passion to our pursuit of the empowering presence of Christ. One of the great contributions of Thomas à Kempis to Christian spirituality is in making us disciples aware that, while we are apprentices and students of Jesus of Nazareth, we must not view him merely as a teacher, ministry supervisor, or life coach. He also desires to be a really good friend to us[18]—and beyond that, to sweep us off our feet![19]

Ignatius of Loyola

In his book *Christian Spirituality,* George Lane defines mysticism as "the direct and experiential awareness of God's presence in the depths of one's person."[20] He goes on to demonstrate how the spirituality promoted by the Spanish monk Ignatius of Loyola (1491–1556) centered in the mystical quest to experience the presence of God in all things, which, in turn, produced a radically new kind of prayer and spirituality.[21]

In addition to being the founder of the Society of Jesus (Jesuits), Ignatius is known for his *Spiritual Exercises*—a series of meditations and prayers designed to enable the retreat participant to experience a mystical union with God that approximates what I refer to as Christ's empowering presence. Prior to Ignatius, there had always been within Christian spirituality a certain tension between the sacred and the secular: prayer and action. "Ignatian" spirituality broke new ground here. By focusing on God's immanent, ubiquitous, ongoing activity in the world, Ignatius came to the conclusion that God is the ultimate worker and that *any work we perform as a result of the union of our will with the will of God can be considered a form of prayer.* In the process, Ignatius seemed to offer a solution to the prayer-work dilemma alluded to above as well as a new understanding of what it means to be spiritual. George Lane explains:

> This notion of God gives rise to a different spirituality. If previous writers conceived of the spiritual as a union with God in interior prayer, Ignatius, being so taken by God's action in the world, was convinced that a person could achieve union with God in action just as well as in contemplation. The operative principle then would be a union of will, man's with God's. Ignatius operated on the principle that to find God's will is to find God, and to do God's will, even in total activity, is to be totally united with God. Thus the man of Ignatian spirituality is one who works with God the worker. And this union with God in action Ignatius calls prayer. What he does here is to expand the notion of prayer to include activity; or better, what he does is recommend that a person "find God in all things." The object is a union with God which for Ignatius can be achieved either in prayer, in the traditional sense, or in action by a union of will with God. And so this "finding God in all things" is the epitome of Ignatian spirituality.[22]

While the language here lacks the "romance rhetoric" and "marital motif" used by other spiritual masters when describing their pursuit of Christ, the concept of Christian spirituality not being limited to what takes place in the monastery chapel or in the monk's cell was an important development. I can't help but think of how Brother Lawrence, about a century later, would speak of communing with Christ as he washed dishes or cooked omelets for his spiritual brothers. Maybe it's a stretch, but I suggest that Ignatius' holistic, pragmatic approach to spirituality has some things in common with the spirituality I'm advocating—a spirituality, focused on the daily pursuit of an empowering presence of Christ, that affects just about *everything we say and do.*

Francis de Sales

The Christian classic entitled *Introduction to the Devout Life,* written by Frances de Sales (1567–1622), overflows with quotable excerpts concerning the pursuit of Christ's empowering presence. De Sales, a priest and bishop, was very involved in the practice of spiritual direction. In fact, it was out of his "concern for the advancement and perfection of individual souls that the *Introduction* grew."[23] As its title suggests, this devotional book was intended to serve as a comprehensive primer on how to achieve spiritual maturity in one's walk with Christ.

Though this devout Roman Catholic bishop was an ardent opponent of the Protestant Reformation, out of which my own spiritual heritage springs, the gist of the pastoral counsel he offered is compelling to me as an evangelical. It strikes me as both pragmatic and passionate at the same time, redolent of a concern for a real relationship with the risen Christ. Hopefully the following set of excerpts (some of them anticipate our later discussions of benefits and means) will give you a feel for the way in which de Sales encouraged his mentorees to settle for nothing less than a continual communion with God.

First, let's be careful to notice how de Sales encouraged his readers to reckon with the reality that God is present everywhere they go.

> God is in all things and all places. There is no place or thing
> in this world where he is not truly present. Just as wherever
> birds fly they always encounter the air, so also wherever we
> go or wherever we are we find God present. Everyone knows

this truth but everyone does not try to bring it home to himself.[24]

Second, we should also pay attention to what de Sales says the effect will be of reminding ourselves all day long that we are actually in the presence of God.

> During the course of the day recall as often as possible . . . that you are in God's presence. Consider what God does and what you are doing. You will see his eyes turned toward you and constantly fixed on you with incomparable love. Then you will say to him: "O God, why do I not look always at you, just as you always look at me? Why do you think so often of me, O my Lord, and why do I think so seldom of you? Where are we, O my soul? God is our true place, and where are we?"[25]

Third, reminiscent of what we heard Brother Lawrence say, de Sales insists that this kind of perpetual remembrance of God throughout the day really is doable for the sincere Christ-follower, despite his or her busy lifestyle.

> If our mind thus habituates itself to intimacy, privacy, and familiarity with God, it will be completely perfumed by his perfections. There is no difficulty in this exercise, as it may be interspersed among all our tasks and duties without any inconvenience, since in this spiritual retirement or amid these interior aspirations we only relax quickly and briefly. This does not hinder but rather assists us greatly in what we do. The pilgrim who takes a little wind to restore his heart and refresh his mouth stops for a while but does not interrupt his journey by doing so. On the contrary, he gains new strength to finish it more quickly and easily since he rests only in order to proceed better.[26]

Finally, we should also pay attention to the beautiful analogy de Sales presses into service to illustrate the spiritual dynamic he prescribes.

> Imitate little children who with one hand hold fast to their father while with the other they gather strawberries or blackberries from the hedges. So too if you gather and handle the good of this world with one hand, you must always hold fast with the other to your heavenly Father's hand and turn toward him from time to time to see if your actions or occupations are pleasing to him.[27]

I trust you agree that these four excerpts from de Sales' *Introduction to the Devout Life* make it very clear that this immediate predecessor to Brother Lawrence viewed the "devout life" as a daily endeavor to experience the life-enhancing presence of God.

Jeremy Taylor

We are discovering in this chapter that the practice of the presence of God has not been limited to any one historical era or geographical locale. From the first century to the seventeenth, and from Jerusalem to Egypt, France, Italy, Holland, Spain, and now England, our survey indicates that spiritually mature Christians the world over and throughout the ages have championed the experience of Christ's empowering presence.

We conclude this chapter with a quick look at the spirituality promoted by Jeremy Taylor (1613–1667), a seventeenth-century Anglican churchman, who wrote several books focusing on the private and public aspects of the religious life.

One of Taylor's works, *The Rule and Exercises of Holy Living,* actually contains a section entitled "The Practice of the Presence of God." In this section, Taylor treats three themes: the several manners (i.e., different ways) in which God is present to us, the rules (i.e., suggestions) for experiencing God's presence, and the benefits of practicing the presence of God. Since we explore the latter two themes in later chapters of this book, we direct our attention now toward one important excerpt from Taylor's discussion of the "several manners of God's presence."

After listing no less than six distinctive ways in which God is present to us, Taylor exhorts his readers to treat the concept of God's nearness with the seriousness it deserves. After being exposed to the language of tender intimacy in the writings of Brother Lawrence, Thomas à Kempis, and Francis de Sales, you will probably be struck by the fact that Taylor takes a more solemn, austere approach when reflecting on the significance of God's presence in our lives. Please don't allow Taylor's bare-knuckled rhetoric or somewhat stilted form of expression to cause you to miss what he has to say about the dynamic of practicing God's presence in our lives. Taylor writes:

> Now the consideration of this great truth is of a very universal use in the whole course of the life of a Christian. All the consequences and effects of it are universal. He that remembers that God stands a witness and a judge beholding every secrecy, besides his impiety must have put on impudence, if he be not much restrained in his temptation to sin. . . . He is a great despiser of God, who sends a boy away when he is going to commit fornication, and yet will dare to do it though he knows God is present, and cannot be sent off: as if the eye of a little boy were more awful than the all-seeing eye of God. He is to be feared in public, He is also to be feared in private: if you go forth, He spies you; if you go in, He sees you: when you light the candle, He observes you; when you put it out, then also God marks you. Be sure that while you are in His sight, you behave yourself as becomes so holy a presence. . . . And certainly if men would always actually consider and really esteem this truth, that God is the great eye of the world, always watching over our actions, and an

ever-open ear to hear all our words, and an unwearied arm ever lifted up to crush a sinner into ruin, it would be the readiest way in the world to make sin to cease from amongst the children of men, and for men to approach to the blessed estate of the saints in heaven, who cannot sin, for they always walk in the presence and behold the face of God.[28]

If nothing else, this passage illustrates how Taylor did not deign to utilize the romance rhetoric or marital motif favored by Thomas à Kempis and Francis de Sales! More important, though, Taylor speaks of the possibility of earthbound believers approaching "the blessed estate of the saints in heaven, who cannot sin, for they always walk in the presence and behold the face of God." It certainly sounds as if Taylor might have had Colossians 3:1–17 in mind. If so, then like every other spiritual master we've looked at so far, he too sees the pursuit of Christ's empowering presence as the key to a "Colossians 3 kind of life"!

Perhaps you're at a place in your spiritual journey where you need to hear that Christ wants to be to you a dear friend with whom you can commune daily. Or it could be that what you really need is a sober reminder of the ongoing presence of a holy God in your life, which, when kept in mind, can serve as a powerful corrective to your sinful proclivities. Whatever you're in need of right now—a sense that you're involved in a sacred romance, or an awe-inspiring, humility-producing, burning-bush experience—the writings of the spiritual masters surveyed in this chapter have what it takes to get the job done!

And there's more to come. In the next chapter, we focus our attention on how some writers of a more recent vintage have likewise joined the chorus of those singing the praise of a daily pursuit of Christ's empowering presence. I think you'll find that these other voices are also quite compelling, perhaps even more so because of their contemporaneity. Turn the page and you'll see what I mean.

— 3 —

"THE PURSUIT" IN THE CONTEMPORARY ERA

How do we cultivate a vibrant Christian spirituality? Dallas Willard suggests "spiritual reading is one of the major sources of light and strength for the disciple of Jesus."[1] I agree and even suggest that in addition to a daily, prayerful reading of the Scriptures, we should nearly always be "nursing" a book that in one way or another enhances our ability to sense God's presence in our lives.

Fortunately, such inspirational works are easy find. The spiritual masters either wrote or caused to be written several significant devotional classics during the early and medieval eras of Christian history. And, certain Christ-followers much nearer to us in time have likewise penned significant works that aim to help Christians cultivate a healthy spirituality. This chapter identifies just a few of these modern authors. What follows is a brief survey of what some especially popular contemporary writers on the spiritual life say about the pursuit of Christ's empowering presence.

Frank Laubach

For most of his life, Frank Laubach (1884–1970) served as a missionary to the Philippines. This long-term American missionary was also an eloquent, passionate champion of the practice of the presence of God. In his various writings on the spiritual life, Laubach recorded the results of his earnest, indefatigable attempts to improve his ability to commune continually with Christ. His audacious, sometimes quirky approach to the pursuit of Christ's empowering presence is intriguing to many. Perhaps it will be to you as well.

Presented below are two lengthy but fascinating excerpts from his writings: one reflects his early experience with "the pursuit," and one illustrates his thinking a little later on. Together, they help us gain a broad overview of his approach to the spiritual life. Early in his spiritual journey toward a "Colossians 3 kind of life," Laubach wrote:

> For the past few days I have been experimenting in a more complete surrender than ever before. I am taking by deliberate act of will, enough time from each hour to give God much thought. Yesterday and today I have made a new adventure, which is not easy to express. I am feeling God in each movement, by an act of will—willing that He shall direct these fingers that now strike this typewriter—willing that He shall pour through my steps as I walk—willing that He shall direct my words as I speak, and my very jaws as I eat!
>
> You will object to this intense introspection. Do not try it, unless you feel dissatisfied with your own relationship with God, but at least allow me to realize all the leadership of God I can. I am disgusted with the pettiness and futility of my unled self. If the way out is not more perfect slavery to God than [sic] what is the way out? Paul speaks of our liberty in Christ. I am trying to be utterly free from everybody, free

from my own self, but completely enslaved to the will of God every moment of the day.

We used to sing a song in the church in Benton which I liked, but which I never practiced until now. It runs:

"Moment by moment I'm kept in His love;
Moment by moment I've life from above;
Looking to Jesus till glory doth shine;
Moment by moment, O Lord, I am Thine."

It is exactly that "moment by moment," every waking moment, surrender, responsiveness, obedience, sensitiveness, pliability, "lost in His love," that I now have the mind-bent to explore with all my might. It means two burning passions: First, to be like Jesus. Second, to respond to God as a violin responds to the bow of the master.[2]

To respond to God as a violin responds to the bow of the master. What a wonderful image! What a great goal! Don't you agree?

Nearly a decade later in his spiritual journey, Laubach's praise for "the pursuit" would prove to be no less effusive. In a subsequent work, we find these words of exhortation:

While a daily devotional hour is vital for saturating our minds with Christ, it is not enough. All during the day, in the chinks of time between the things we find ourselves obliged to do, there are moments when our minds ask: "What next?" In these chinks of time, ask Him:

"Lord, think Thy thoughts in my mind. What is on Thy mind for me to do now?"

When we ask Christ, "What's next?" we tune in and give Him a chance to pour His ideas through our enkindled imagination. If we persist, it becomes a habit. It takes some effort, but it is worth a million times what it costs. It is possible for everybody, everywhere. Even if we are surrounded by throngs of people, we can continue to talk silently with our invisible Friend. We need not close our eyes nor change our position nor move our lips.[3]

Did you notice in these two quotes how Laubach's commitment to the pursuit of Christ's empowering presence not only remained unwavering but also seemed to grow stronger as time passed? Perhaps you also noticed how the *descriptive* tenor of his earlier writing eventually morphed into something more *prescriptive*. This change in tone is not unusual among those who have taken "the pursuit" seriously. Having discovered what they believe is the key to living a "Colossians 3 kind of life," they can't help but *prescribe* this approach to Christian spirituality to everyone who will listen!

A. W. Tozer

The writings of pastor and author A. W. Tozer (1897–1963) profoundly affected my spiritual journey when I first came across them in the late 1970s. I had been a Christian for only a couple of years when I stumbled upon *The Pursuit of God*. Reading that book awakened the mystic within me—it made me hungry for God.

In this Christian classic, Tozer alludes to the practice of the presence of God in several places. In one excerpt, Tozer indicates that the pursuit of Christ's empowering presence involves a ceaseless beholding of Jesus with the eyes of the heart.

> Believing, then, is directing the heart's attention to Jesus. It is lifting the mind to "behold the Lamb of God," and never ceasing that beholding for the rest of our lives. At first this may be difficult, but it becomes easier as we look steadily at His wondrous Person, quietly and without strain. Distractions may hinder, but once the heart is committed to Him, after each brief excursion away from Him the attention will return again and rest upon Him like a wandering bird coming back to its window.[4]

In another excerpt, Tozer expands upon the idea of a ceaseless beholding of Christ, indicating that *this particular spiritual exercise is at the heart of all the other spiritual disciplines in which we might engage.*

> I do not want to leave the impression that the ordinary means of grace have no value. They most assuredly have. Private prayer should be practiced by every Christian. Long periods of Bible meditation will purify our gaze and direct it; church attendance will enlarge our outlook and increase our love for others. Service and work and activity; all are good and should be engaged in by every Christian. But at the bottom of all these things, giving meaning to them, will be the inward habit of beholding God. A new set of eyes (so to speak) will develop within us enabling us to be looking at God while our outward eyes are seeing the scenes of this passing world.[5]

Isn't that good stuff? A later chapter of *Christ's Empowering Presence* focuses on the many benefits "the pursuit" produces in our lives. There, we'll find that Tozer has much more to say about this foundational approach to Christian spirituality. For now, it's enough that we catch the "vision" that Tozer, the evangelical mystic, endeavored to cast before his readers: It's possible for Christians to come to the place where we "see" that to which we were previously oblivious, to develop the "inward habit of beholding God," regardless of what goes on around us.

Leslie Weatherhead

Though not a large volume, *The Transforming Friendship,* written by English churchman Leslie Weatherhead (1893–1976), is an extremely powerful piece of devotional literature. Weatherhead defines the essence of Christianity as "the acceptance of the gift of the friendship of Jesus."[6] He argues that, because Jesus was such a compelling, charismatic figure whose very presence seemed to have a transforming effect on those who shared his company, a real friendship with Jesus will necessarily be a transforming one.[7] To convince his readers that a transforming friendship with Jesus is a real possibility in our own era, Weatherhead poses a series of rhetorical questions that illustrate what he thinks a real "friendship" with the risen Christ would entail.

> Is it a real fact, practicable for everyday life in the twentieth century, that we may have communion with Jesus Christ as really as we have communion with our earthly friends? Can we know that same Jesus of Nazareth who walked about in Galilee two thousand years ago? I do not mean can we treasure His words, can we follow His way of life, can we, following His example, be heroic as He was, can we benefit by His ideas; I do not mean can we imaginatively reproduce a picture of Him clearly enough to form a substitute for His actual presence; but can we really meet Him, know Him, commune with Himself?[8]

Apparently, Weatherhead has in mind the possibility of contemporary Christians actually communing with the real, risen Jesus of Nazareth—rather than with some idealized version of him! This transforming friendship Weatherhead portrays is clearly the experience I refer to as the empowering presence of Christ.

> What Jesus once was, He is eternally. He comes to us, not only in His temple, or in the room when the door is shut, but as He came to Mary and Martha in the midst of household tasks, and as He came to Peter mending his nets and doing his daily work; and He comes with the same offer, the offer of His transforming friendship. There are no conditions save the imaginative faith to believe that He is, and that fellowship with Him is possible.
>
> Can we enter into this friendship? We can. We can, as Brother Lawrence said, "practise the Presence of God," but

the only way I know of practising the presence of God is by practising the presence of Jesus, who makes God credible and real, and entering into the transforming friendship which He offers.[9]

Besides supporting the idea that practicing the presence of God and pursuing Christ's empowering presence ultimately amount to the same thing, this passage does something else. Evidently speaking from personal experience, Weatherhead assures us that we can actually do this: we can experience a transformational friendship with the real Jesus. Indeed, in yet another excerpt from *The Transforming Friendship,* Weatherhead provides a methodology for getting such a friendship started.

Try it. Sit down quietly for ten minutes every day for a month. Let your mind go out to Jesus. Think about Him. Believe that what He once was He eternally is. What He was for men and women years ago, He is for you today. All His followers would guarantee that you will find Him no ghost, but a Friend; no mere memory of long ago, but a living personal Savior whose friendship will transform your whole nature.[10]

I interrupt our survey just long enough to underscore an important implication of Weatherhead's emphasis upon the dynamic continuity between the historical Jesus of Nazareth and the heavenly Christ, whose empowering presence we seek to experience daily. In Colossians 3:1–4, the apostle Paul encouraged his readers to set their minds on the resurrected and ascended Christ. Paul went on, in Colossians 3:5–17, to indicate the transformative effect this practice would have upon their lives. It's important to point out that Paul, like Weatherhead, had in mind as the object of our spiritual gaze the real, risen Jesus who now resides at the right hand of God—not some mythical, idealized version of him. *This is an important detail, lest we attempt to forge a relationship with an illusion: a domesticated*

Jesus we've created in our own image, whose friendship will prove to be neither empowering nor transforming!

For it to be truly transformational, our friendship must be with the same Jesus who befriended Peter, Mary, Martha, Lazarus, Zacchaeus, Nicodemus, the woman at the well, and the thief on the cross. This Jesus was gracious toward his friends, but also demanding. He loved people the way he found them, but too much to allow them to stay that way. Jesus was not beyond stretching his friends to make them better, to help them become the kind of people they, deep inside, really wanted to be.

In other words, the real Jesus has an agenda. Will he function as a true friend? Yes. Can we succeed at turning him into some sort of divine butler? No. We should therefore be warned: for all our talk about knowing Jesus as a dear friend, the reality is that this approach to Christian spirituality will sometimes take us places we're not always sure we want to go. We can rest assured, however, that Christ's goal for us is always a good one: a "Colossians 3 kind of life"![11]

Dallas Willard

Dallas Willard is a professor of philosophy at the University of Southern California. He is also a prolific author of books relating not only to philosophy but to Christian spirituality as well. Though Willard appears reluctant to use the phrase "the practice of the presence of God," I believe his writings reflect a profound appreciation for this concept.

In one of his most recent books, *Knowing Christ Today: Why We Can Trust Spiritual Knowledge,* Willard speaks of the possibility of living one's life with a "Christ focus," one aspect of which involves "the practice of Christ's constant presence."[12] He also writes in this book of our need to open ourselves to the "Presence,"[13] thus achieving something he refers to as the "with God" life.[14]

In his earlier books, Willard goes into much more detail about what we call "the pursuit." For instance, in *Renovation of the Heart,* Willard contends there are six basic aspects in our lives (thought, feeling, choice, body, social context, and soul), and "the ideal of the spiritual life in the Christian understanding is one where all of the essential parts of the human self are effectively organized around God, as they are restored and sustained by him."[15] The implied idea is that the goal of Christian spirituality is a life centered in God. Because our thought life is one of our essential aspects, and because what we think about most will influence our feelings, choices, and so forth, we should not be surprised to find Willard encouraging the practice of thinking often of God.

> To bring the mind to dwell intelligently upon God as he is presented in his Word will have the effect of causing us to love God passionately, and this love will in turn bring us to think of God steadily.[16]

> The intention to be formed is to have the great God and Father of our Lord Jesus Christ a constant presence in our mind, crowding out every false idea or destructive image, all misinformation about God, and every crooked inference or belief.[17]

Furthermore, in other places within *Renovation of the Heart,* Willard speaks of the importance of pursuing Christ in particular. He introduces the idea of "the pursuit" this way:

> We therefore live in "hot pursuit" of Jesus Christ. "My soul followeth hard after thee," the psalmist called out (Psalm 63:8, KJV). And Paul's panting cry was, "That I may know Him, and the power of His resurrection and the fellowship of His sufferings, being conformed to His death" in order to participate in the life of his resurrection (Philippians 3:10–11

[NASB]). What are we to say of anyone who thinks they have something more important to do than that?[18]

Why is Christ so important to the spiritual life? Willard contends that "the pursuit" is crucial to our being able to go beyond mere head knowledge of God to an actual experience of him.

> "Knowledge of the Holy One is understanding," Proverbs 9:10 [NASB] concludes. "Knowledge" in biblical language never refers to what we today call "head knowledge," but always *to experiential involvement* with what is known—to actual engagement with it. Thus when Jesus defines the eternal life that he gives to his people as "that they might know thee, the only true God, and Jesus Christ, whom thou has sent" (John 17:3, KJV), he is speaking of the grace of constant, close interaction with the Trinitarian being of God that Jesus brings into the lives of those who seek and find him.[19]

Finally, in complete accord with other spiritual masters, Willard insists that a daily pursuit of Christ's empowering presence will have a dramatic impact upon the entirety of our lives (rather than just what we do on Sundays)!

> The second aspect of discipleship concerns all the details of what, for lack of a better term, we call our "secular," or "non-churchy" life. How do you run a business? How do you live with your parents or a mate, or raise a family? How do you get along with neighbors, participate in government, get an education, engage in the cultural life of your society? These too are matters in which we are to be constantly learning how Jesus would lead our lives if he were we. He would do those things if he were we. And they are not just matters of keeping his commandments, though they presuppose that. In these matters of ordinary human existence also, Jesus is our constant teacher and we his constant apprentices. "He walks

with me and he talks with me," as the old hymn says, about all these matters.[20]

So far, our focus has been on Willard's *Knowing Christ Today* and *Renovation of the Heart.* In an even earlier work, *Hearing God: Developing a Conversational Relationship with God,* Willard focuses, as the book's title implies, even more precisely on the possibility of our developing an intimate, interactive, ongoing experience of God. We've already come across the idea that God desires that his people experience a friendship with him that is close, personal, and enduring. Willard echoes this idea in *Hearing God,* providing biblical support for it in the process.

> God has created us for intimate friendship with himself—both now and forever. This is the Christian viewpoint. It is made clear throughout the Bible, especially in such passages as Exodus 29:43–46 and 33:11, Psalm 23, Isaiah 41:8, John 15:14 and Hebrews 13:5–6. As with all close personal relationships, we can surely count on God to speak to each of us when and as it is appropriate.[21]

Willard proceeds in *Hearing God* to speak of the tremendous importance an "ongoing conversation" with God will have upon our spiritual lives. And once again, he alludes to several biblical examples, evidently in a bid to marshal support for the idea that such a lifestyle should be the norm rather than the exception.

> Today I continue to believe that people are meant to live in an ongoing conversation with God, speaking and being spoken to. Rightly understood I believe that this can be abundantly verified in experience. God's visits to Adam and Eve in the Garden, Enoch's walks with God and the face-to-face conversations between Moses and Jehovah are all commonly regarded as highly exceptional moments in the religious history of humankind. Aside from their obviously unique historical role, however, they are not meant to be exceptional

at all. Rather they are examples of the normal human life God intended for us:

> God's indwelling his people through personal presence and fellowship. Given who we are by basic nature, we live—really live—only through God's regular speaking in our souls and thus "by every word that comes from out of the mouth of God."[22]

In a third excerpt from *Hearing God,* Willard emphasizes the important truth that the personal relationship with God he describes will involve much more than management of our sins. Willard's concern is not to deny the importance of what Christ has done to make it possible for sinners to go to heaven when they die, but rather to help us understand that Jesus desires to empower all of his apprentices to become less sinful here and now! And how does Jesus accomplish this transformation of his followers? It's with this question in mind that Willard encourages us to think more deeply about what it means to have Jesus as a *friend.*

> Sometimes today it seems that our personal relationship with God is treated as no more than a mere arrangement or understanding that Jesus and his Father have about us. Our personal relationship then only means that each believer has his or her own unique account in heaven, which allows them to draw on the merits of Christ to pay their sin bills. Or possibly it means that God's general providence for his creation is adequate to provide for each person.
>
> But who does not think there should be much more to a personal relationship than that? A mere benefactor, however powerful, kind and thoughtful, is not the same thing as a *friend.* Jesus says, "I have called you friends" (John 15:15) and "Look, I am with you every minute, even to the end of the age" (Matthew 28:20, paraphrase; cf. Hebrews 13:5–6).[23]

Thus, we find ourselves, once again, coming across the concept of a *transforming friendship*. Could the pervasiveness of this theme in the writings of so many spiritual masters be evidence that the pursuit of Christ's empowering presence really is at the heart of Christian spirituality?

Jan Johnson

I met Jan Johnson in the summer of 2002 at the "Spirituality and Ministry" seminar referred to previously. Jan is a friendly, vivacious woman of God who writes books, provides spiritual direction, and speaks to women and other groups about real-life issues.

One of the many books Johnson has authored is entitled *Enjoying the Presence of God.* This is a valuable volume for folks such as you and me—pilgrims just starting out in our pursuit of Christ's empowering presence. It's filled with many practical suggestions for how contemporary Christians can incorporate this ancient spiritual exercise into our daily lives. At this point in our study, I draw your attention to just one excerpt from Johnson's book. In this quote, she provides an overall description of "the pursuit" that is both accessible and inspirational.

> An awareness of God can flow through our day the way blood circulates through the body, replenishing it with nutrients and oxygen. We pay attention to God, conscious that He may be speaking to us. His presence begins to permeate our lives—through thoughts, feelings, dreams, activities, and in-between moments.
>
> Practicing God's presence moves His companionship beyond church gatherings, before-meal graces, and quiet times to infiltrate the ordinary moments of life. Keeping company with God this way transforms tasks such as building circuit boards into acts of worship because we know at whose feet we sit for the rest of our lives.[24]

In my mind, the influence of Brother Lawrence is discernable here. Needless to say, Brother Lawrence is not exactly one of our contemporaries, but Johnson has succeeded in portraying the practice of the presence of God in a way that brings Brother Lawrence into our own era. Is this merely the result of Johnson's literary skill, or is it also an indication that Brother Lawrence's approach to spirituality possesses an enduring quality, which evidences its cruciality to a sincere and transformative walk with Christ?

Richard Foster

In his excellent book *Prayer: Finding the Heart's True Home*, Richard Foster, university professor and author of many works on Christian spirituality, also refers to the practice of the presence of God. In fact, he does us a great service by pulling together some powerful descriptions of this holy habit that have been put forward over the years by a few spiritual masters not treated in this historical survey. For example, as the lead-in to a chapter entitled "Unceasing Prayer," Foster presses into service the following quote from the seventh-century monk Isaac the Syrian:

> When the Spirit has come to reside in someone, that person cannot stop praying; for the Spirit prays without ceasing in him. No matter if he is asleep or awake, prayer is going on in his heart all the time. He may be eating or drinking, he may be resting or working—the incense of prayer will ascend spontaneously from his heart. The slightest stirring of his heart is like a voice which sings in silence and in secret to the Invisible.[25]

Foster then formally begins his chapter on unceasing prayer with a paragraph in which he not only describes the practice I'm prescribing but also says, in effect, that it is indispensable to one's walk with Christ.

I want to tell you of a wonderful way of living always in God's presence. I cannot witness that I have entered fully into this life of perpetual communion with the Father, but I have caught enough glimpses that I know it to be the best, the finest, the fullest way of living.[26]

How does one maintain a sense of "perpetual communion" with God? Foster's answer: the practice of unceasing prayer. Then, before writing anything else, he cites no less than six spiritual masters who refer to this practice in their writings, three of whom haven't been included in our survey.

Ordinary folk throughout the ages tell us it is possible. Brother Lawrence shares simply, "There is no mode of life in the world more pleasing and more full of delight than continual conversation with God." Saint John of the Ladder advises, "Let the memory of Jesus combine with your breath." Julian of Norwich says frankly, "Prayer unites the soul to God." Kallistos, a Byzantine spiritual writer, teaches, "Unceasing prayer consists in an unceasing invocation of the name of God." It was said of Saint Francis that he "seemed not so much a man praying as prayer itself made man." And Frank Laubach reports, "Oh, this thing of keeping in constant touch with God, of making him the object of my thought and the companion of my conversations, is the most amazing thing I ever ran across."[27]

Elsewhere in this same chapter, Foster cites Thomas Kelly's well-known reference to the experience of Christ's empowering presence—a reference that Kelly included in his work *A Testament of Devotion*.

There is a way of ordering our mental life on more than one level at once. On one level we may be thinking, discussing, seeing, calculating, meeting all the demands of external affairs. But deep within, behind the scenes, at a profounder level, we may also be in prayer and adoration, song and worship and a gentle receptiveness to divine breathings.[28]

A gentle receptiveness to divine breathings. What a powerful image! What sincere follower of Jesus doesn't want to experience growth in this regard? I'm convinced that all of us have been "wired" by God to want to engage in a daily pursuit of Christ's empowering presence.

John Ortberg

I conclude this chapter's survey of contemporary devotional authors who have made significant references to "the pursuit" by alluding to the work of pastor and author John Ortberg. Ortberg's *The Life You've Always Wanted: Spiritual Disciplines for Ordinary People* is one of the best of the popular books on Christian spirituality on the market today.[29] However, while Ortberg merely flirts with the idea of Christ's empowering presence in *The Life You've Always Wanted,* he marries himself to the concept in a subsequent work entitled *God Is Closer Than You Think.* Early in this great book, Ortberg explains:

> God is closer than we think. He is never farther than a prayer away. All it takes is the barest effort, the lift of a finger. Every moment—this moment right now, as you read these words—is the "one timeless moment" of divine endowment, of life with God.[30]

Throughout the remainder of this work, Ortberg repeatedly refers to the pursuit of Christ's empowering presence, and he does so in a variety of ways. Like Richard Foster, Ortberg sometimes cites the work of a spiritual master. Other times, he simply expresses what is in his own heart. The following excerpts from *God Is Closer Than You Think* not only present a clearer understanding of what's involved in "the pursuit" but they also make me, whenever I read them, want to persist in it. I hope they have the same effect upon you. Ortberg writes:

The teaching of Scripture is that God really is present right here, right now. . . . The Spirit of God is available to you and me: flowing all the time, welling up within us, quenching our unsatisfied desires, overflowing to refresh those around us. He is at work all the time, in every place. And every once in a while, somebody somewhere shows up.[31]

I want to be that somebody who shows up! Don't you? Ortberg continues:

Spiritual growth, in a sense, is simply increasing our capacity to experience the presence of God. Brother Lawrence wrote: "The most holy and necessary practice in our spiritual life is the presence of God. That means finding constant pleasure in His divine company, speaking humbly and lovingly with him in all seasons, at every moment, without limiting the conversation in any way."[32]

To what degree have you experienced genuine spiritual growth so far in your walk with Christ? Is it time to begin engaging in "the pursuit" in a more earnest manner?

Ortberg goes on to wonder aloud:

Maybe ordinary days aren't "ordinary" at all, but part of the required course to develop wonder-filled eyes and praise-fluent tongues. William Barry writes, "Whether we are aware of it or not, at every moment of our existence we are encountering God, Father, Son, and Holy Spirit, who is trying to catch our attention, trying to draw us into a reciprocal conscious relationship." Perhaps our capacity to pay attention to God—like the capacity to lift weights or speak Spanish—only gets stronger when it gets exercised.[33]

On the one hand, this quote can fill us with hope: our capacity to pay attention to God, with practice, becomes stronger over time. On the other hand, the quote also presents us with a challenge: Are we willing to do what it takes? Actually, I'm not sure if I like this quote or not!

Then again, what are we supposed to do? In this final but poignant passage, Ortberg pretty much bottom-lines us. He essentially asserts that we really aren't Jesus' disciples if we haven't made the decision to spend every day of the rest of our lives engaged in "the pursuit."

> The decision that makes us disciples is choosing to be always with Jesus so we can learn continually from Jesus how to be fully like him.[34]

Choosing to be always with Jesus so we can learn how to be fully like him. Isn't this what the pursuit of Christ's empowering presence is about? What do you think? Could Ortberg be correct in his claim that a decision to participate passionately in "the pursuit" is integral to a healthy, vibrant Christian discipleship?

Actually, I'm getting ahead of myself. It's in part two of this book that I encourage you to form a sturdy intention to follow the lead of the spiritual mentors we've been looking at and to begin your own pursuit of Christ's empowering presence. The primary goal of the first three chapters has merely been to cast a vision before you of what pursuing the empowering presence of Christ would involve.

Hopefully I've also succeeded at a secondary goal: to provide a collection of inspiring quotes that may be of value to you in the future. The truth is that, despite the importance of "the pursuit" to the Christian life, it's easy for sincere but hurried Christ-followers to become so distracted in our discipleship that we fail to—as Ortberg puts it—"show up." Should this ever happen to you, I hope you will have the presence of mind to reach for this book and begin reading from it again. The ancient spiritual exercise we've been examining does indeed have an enduring quality about it, as do the references to it penned by Christianity's most anointed spiritual masters.

And there are more inspiring quotes to come! Let's proceed now to the next phase in the spiritual journey we're taking together: a leg in the expedition where, hopefully, we become thoroughly convinced that "the pursuit" really is at the heart of Christian spirituality and, as a result, make up our minds to begin participating in it.

PART TWO

INTENTION:

WHY WE SHOULD COMMIT
OURSELVES TO THE PURSUIT OF
CHRIST'S EMPOWERING PRESENCE

4

SUPPORT FOR "THE PURSUIT" IN THE OLD TESTAMENT SCRIPTURES

So, how eager are you at this point in our journey to begin your own pursuit of Christ's empowering presence? To encourage his readers to believe that God himself yearns for his people to do this very thing, Richard Foster writes:

> God has graciously allowed me to catch a glimpse into his heart, and I want to share what I have seen. Today the heart of God is an open wound of love. He aches over our distance and preoccupation. He mourns that we do not draw near to him. He grieves that we have forgotten him. He weeps over our obsession with muchness and manyness. He longs for our presence.
>
> And he is inviting you—and me—to come home, to come home where we belong, to come home to that for which we were created. His arms are stretched out wide to receive us. His heart is enlarged to take us in.
>
> For too long we have been in a far country: a country of noise and hurry and crowds, a country of climb

and push and shove, a country of frustration and fear and intimidation. And he welcomes us home: home to serenity and peace and joy, home to friendship and fellowship and openness, home to intimacy and acceptance and affirmation.[1]

My primary objective in part two of this book is to provide a variety of reasons why you should make it your intention to do precisely what Foster advocates: *come home to a sense of God's presence.* However, if you strive, as I do, to live under the authority of God's Word, you might be wondering if this business of practicing the presence of God really does possess biblical warrant. Thus, in the next two chapters I highlight *the presence of God* as a theme that runs throughout the Scriptures and "the pursuit" as an approach to spirituality that is enjoined upon all of us by the biblical authors (and the Holy Spirit who inspired them). A secondary aim is to provide, once again, a plethora of quotes—this time from the Scriptures—to which you can turn in the days, weeks, months, and years ahead when a bit of fresh inspiration is needed to remain engaged in the pursuit of Christ's empowering presence.

The precise focus of this chapter is the way in which "the pursuit" is referred to in the Old Testament. By way of overview, we've seen how Richard Woods, in his book *Christian Spirituality,* argues that the spirituality at work in the Old Testament community of faith centered on the theme of God being present to his people.[2] Indeed, as Woods makes clear, the idea that the real presence of God could be experienced by *anyone* within the Israelite community ultimately differentiated Israel's faith from that of the nations round about her.[3] According to this assessment, though the religious practices of ancient Israel did eventually become institutionalized and ritualized, it was not always that way, nor did it remain so forever. No, in the beginning, the spirituality practiced by the Old Testament saints was just as intimately interactive as was that of the great Christian spiritual masters we surveyed in part one of this work. And as the

Christian era drew near, the Jewish prophets could be heard calling for a spirituality that was anything but institutional and ritualistic.

All of this explains Woods' use of the phrase "the practice of the presence of God" in his depiction of the spirituality of the Old Testament believer. He writes, "Israel's God chose to inhabit the interior recesses of the human spirit—consciousness, memory, and the attunement of wills. The pinnacle of religious observance thus came to be neither pilgrimage nor sacrifice but recollection—the sharpening of inner and loving attentiveness, the practice of the presence of God."[4]

In the remainder of this chapter, I draw your attention to a number of Old Testament texts that seem to support Woods' contention that even during this earlier era of salvation history God's desire was for his people to experience an empowering sense of his presence. Clearly the survey presented here cannot be exhaustive. An entire book could very well be devoted to such a task! Instead, my much simpler approach will, first of all, provide a basic survey of the major eras of Old Testament history, highlighting from each era a representative passage or two that demonstrates the importance of the theme of God's presence to the biblical story. Second, I also present a brief review of the prayers and songs of praise we find in the Book of Psalms, once again focusing on the theme of God's presence. My hope is that a perusal of the many biblical passages presented below will convince you that "the pursuit" is indeed a spiritual exercise that finds tacit support in the Old Testament Scriptures.

God's Presence as a Prominent Theme in the Old Testament Narrative as a Whole

Woods' argument concerning the spirituality at work in the Old Testament community of faith implies that God's presence was an integral aspect of this phase of the biblical story of redemption. Is this idea valid? Let's find out for ourselves.

The Primeval Era

One way to understand Genesis 1–11, which scholars refer to as the Bible's "primeval prologue," is as a masterful introduction to the Scriptures' dramatic story of redemption. Why the biblical narrative should be considered *a tale of universal redemption* is precisely what the first eleven chapters of Genesis explains. Following the creation account presented in Genesis 1 and 2, the actual fall of humanity is related in Genesis 3:1–6, with its disastrous aftereffects vividly described in Genesis 3:7–11:9. Though once upon a time human beings were privy to a wonderful experience of God's unmediated presence that enlivened every aspect of existence (spiritual, psychological, marital, sociological, and physiological), all this is gone by the time the primeval prologue concludes! In other words, the main message of the first few chapters of the Bible is how the world went wrong and why we therefore now find ourselves feeling so existentially *estranged* from God and, as a result, estranged from nature, our own selves, and one another.

Now try to imagine a reader, completely unfamiliar with the biblical drama, picking up the Bible and reading it for the first time. As she concludes her reading of Genesis 1:1–11:9, she's likely to shake her head and wonder, *What will God do now that humanity seems so totally and irrevocably estranged from him?*

As she continues to read, she finds that Genesis 11:10–31 presents a genealogy that ultimately leads to a man named Terah and his son Abram. In Genesis 11:32, she discovers that Terah dies, leaving the focus on Abram alone. Our reader might then wonder, *Who is this fellow Abram, and what does he have to do with whatever God has planned for this world gone horribly awry?* Then in Genesis 12, she discovers the biblical answer to both of her queries: with the divine call of Abram to become the father of a new nation, the biblical story of redemption officially begins. God will use this particular nation to bring blessing to all the nations of the earth (Genesis 12:1–3; see also Isaiah 49:1–6).

Thus, our theoretical reader will eventually discover that *the biblical story is all about the healing of the breach between God and humanity*. What had been lost as a result of the fall—the ability to commune with God daily in the garden (compare Genesis 3:8 with 3:23–24)—has been regained by the promised descendant ("seed") of Abraham, making it possible for humanity to once again gain access to the unmediated, life-giving presence of God (see Genesis 22:18; Acts 3:24–26; Galatians 3:16, 26–29; Revelation 21:1–3). In this way, the primeval prologue speaks to us of the vital importance of God's presence. The biblical story is all about God making it possible for his estranged creation to "come home" to him!

The Era of the Patriarchs

The patriarchal narratives (stories related to Abraham, Isaac, and Jacob) seem to carry forward the theme of God's presence. The Book of Genesis portrays God making some wonderful promises to Abraham and his son Isaac in an amazingly intimate, interactive manner. For instance, passages such as Genesis 17:1–22 and 18:1–33, which record whole conversations between God and Abraham, imply some sort of an especially personal encounter as the venue. Passages such as Genesis 26:1–6 and 26:24 indicate that Isaac likewise experienced God's presence in some remarkable and unmistakable ways.

However, it's also true that the biblical story goes on to present Isaac's son, the rascally Jacob, as a potential wrench in the messianic machinery. Would God be willing to work with such a strong-willed, conniving person, whose name means "deceiver"? Amazingly, the answer is yes. According to the pivotal story related in Genesis

32:22–30, Jacob wrestled with God (in the form of an angel) as with a man. And it was to Jacob that God made the following amazing promise regarding his presence:

> I am with you and will watch over you wherever you go, and
> I will bring you back to this land. I will not leave you until I
> have done what I have promised you. (Genesis 28:15)

I want to suggest that the biblical author intended for this powerful promise of God's empowering presence, given its literary context, to be viewed as the overarching theme of the patriarchal narratives as a whole. The patriarchs are presented to Bible readers as imperfect persons who were, nevertheless, very familiar with God's manifest presence. A restored communion with God seems to be the goal of grace.

The Era of the Exodus

Moving forward, according to the biblical narrative, the descendants of Abraham, Isaac, and Jacob eventually found themselves living as slaves in Egypt. The Lord sent Moses to deliver his people from the Egyptian Pharaoh's oppressive rule. Moses hadn't been leading the people of Israel very long, however, when he recognized that the task to which he had been called was far beyond his ability to pull off in his own strength. He needed assurance that God's empowering presence would be with him. There was, however, a problem. God, in response to the hard-heartedness previously displayed by the Israelites, had already indicated there was no way he would personally accompany Moses and his charges; their persistent sinfulness would likely provoke God to destroy them along the way (Exodus 33:1–5)!

But Moses prayed, beseeching God to tell him what kind of assistance he could count on. God's response to this prayer was simple and sublime, redolent of grace:

> The Lord replied, "My Presence will go with you, and I will give you rest." (Exodus 33:14)

There's a sense in which all the drama in the ensuing accounts of the wilderness wanderings and the eventual conquest of Canaan revolve around this theme of God endeavoring to be present to a hardheaded, stiff-necked people. Perhaps this explains why we read of Moses spending so much time in prayer!

The Era of the Judges

Once the people of Israel had conquered the land of Canaan, their hearts grew cold toward God and the law he had given them through Moses. Everyone did as he or she saw fit (Judges 17:6; 21:25), and so the Israelites did evil in the eyes of the Lord (Judges 2:11; 3:7; 3:12; 4:1; 6:1; 10:6; 13:1). The Book of Judges chronicles several "defection-discipline-deliverance" cycles that occurred during this especially turbulent period in Israel's history. Really, it's the same dramatic tension we've seen before. This is a story of the Lord's commitment to be providentially present to a people whose hearts are prone to wander from him. Each episode of divine discipline followed by divine deliverance tells us something about God: though too holy to tolerate sin, he's amazingly responsive to the dynamic of sincere repentance. Whenever his people genuinely turn their hearts toward him, he rushes toward them in a saving, restorative manner!

Especially inspiring is the story of God calling fearful, intimidated Gideon into service as one of Israel's deliverers. In the process of recruiting this unlikely hero, God gave Gideon some wonderful promises regarding his empowering presence.

> When the angel of the Lord appeared to Gideon, he said, "The Lord is with you, mighty warrior."
>
> "But sir," Gideon replied, "if the Lord is with us, why has all this happened to us? Where are all his wonders that our fathers told us about when they said, 'Did not the Lord

bring us up out of Egypt?' But now the Lord has abandoned us and put us into the hand of Midian."

The Lord turned to him and said, "Go in the strength you have and save Israel out of Midian's hand. Am I not sending you?"

"But Lord," Gideon asked, "how can I save Israel? My clan is the weakest in Manasseh, and I am the least in my family."

The Lord answered, "I will be with you, and you will strike down all the Midianites together." (Judges 6:12–16)

Isn't there a sense in which all of us can relate to Gideon? Don't we all want to believe in our heart that God hasn't given up on us, that he knows what we're going through and still sees something noble in us—even when our actions of late have been anything but noble? I believe the biblical author was counting on the fact that deep inside all of us there exists a resilient desire to believe that *no matter how sinful we've been, God still wants to be with us.* This is precisely what makes the story so inspiring.

The Era of the Monarchy

Even though Israel's insistence on obtaining a king in order to be like all the other nations (1 Samuel 8:1–5) was interpreted by God as a rejection of his loving lordship (1 Samuel 8:6–7), once it occurred and the monarchy was established, we read of God being very involved in the selection process. After Saul proved unwilling to be directed by God, the Lord gave the prophet Samuel the task of locating and anointing Saul's replacement: a man who would be much more sensitive, so to speak, to divine breathings (1 Samuel 13:14). First Samuel 16:1–13 tells the story of Samuel identifying a young shepherd named David as Saul's divinely chosen successor. This passage also indicates that David's anointing involved a close encounter with God's empowering presence: "So Samuel took the horn of oil and anointed him in the presence of his brothers, and from that day on the Spirit of the LORD came upon David in power" (1 Samuel 16:13).

What was the result of this empowering experience with God's Spirit? The Bible is clear: David's great success as Israel's king came because the Lord was *with* him (1 Samuel 18:14; 2 Samuel 5:10; 1 Chronicles 11:9).

Unfortunately, though, the story goes on to tell us that a united monarchy didn't last very long. David's kingdom was split into two during the reign of his grandson Rehoboam. Thereafter, the northern kingdom—Israel—with its eventual capital in Samaria, was ruled by a series of more or less wicked, idolatrous kings, while the southern kingdom—Judah—with its capital in Jerusalem, was ruled by a series of Davidic descendants who were also more or less idolatrous. It's important to note the way in which some of Judah's best kings are described. Like David, it was said of Judah's finest kings that the Lord was graciously *with* them (2 Kings 18:5–7; 2 Chronicles 15:8–9)! Thus, it appears that the theme of God's presence is at the very heart of the story of Israel's monarchy, during both its unified and divided phases.

The Era of the Exile

From the very beginning of their sojourn in the land of promise, the people of Israel had been warned by God that should they break the terms of their covenant with him, then they would be uprooted from the land and scattered among the nations (Deuteronomy 4:23–27; 28:58–64; 29:24–28). Despite subsequent warnings provided by her prophets, the Israelites did break faith with Yahweh, persisting in the sins of idolatry, immorality, and injustice. So, God made good on his promise of judgment. In 2 Kings 17:7–23, the biblical author describes the exile of the ten northern tribes that occurred as a result of the Assyrian conquest circa 722 BC. In the process, he speaks repeatedly of the people being *removed from God's presence* (see 2 Kings 17:18, 20, and 23).

Later, around 586 BC, the southern kingdom was conquered by the Babylonian king Nebuchadnezzar, thus initiating what's known as the Babylonian captivity. It's interesting that as the prophet Jeremiah refers to this act of divine discipline, he repeatedly uses the language of *banishment* (Jeremiah 8:3; 16:15; 23:8; 23:12; 24:9; 25:10; 27:10; 27:15; 29:14; 32:37). Furthermore, keeping passages such as Jeremiah 7:15, 15:1, 23:39, and 52:3 in mind, it's clear that Jeremiah envisioned not just a banishment from the land of promise, but a banishment from God's life-giving, shalom-producing *presence* as well!

And yet the story doesn't end there. During an early phase of the exile, the Holy Spirit moved the weeping prophet to write a letter to leaders of the Jewish captives, who had already been taken to Babylon. In the letter, Jeremiah encouraged these exiles to settle down in Babylon and, in various ways, to get on with their lives (Jeremiah 29:1–7). Then came a word of promise—a famous, oft-cited promise that had to do with God's *presence:*

> This is what the LORD says: "When seventy years are completed for Babylon, I will come to you and fulfill my gracious promise to bring you back to this place. For I know the plans I have for you," declares the LORD, "plans to prosper you and not to harm you, plans to give you hope and a future. Then you will call upon me and come and pray to me, and I will listen to you. You will seek me and find me when you seek me with all your heart. I will be found by you," declares the LORD, "and will bring you back from captivity. I will gather you from all the nations and places where I have banished you," declares the LORD, "and will bring you back to the place from which I carried you into exile." (Jeremiah 29:10–14)

So, once again we find in the biblical story the theme of God's great desire not to be estranged from his covenant partners. This unrelenting eagerness of God to be with his people is really quite remarkable, isn't it?

The Postexilic Era of Return

The Old Testament story concludes with God fulfilling his promise to eventually bring a remnant of Jews back to the land from which they had been banished. Jeremiah 31 makes it abundantly clear that this was not, however, just a geographical move. Instead, it constituted an end to the people's spiritual estrangement from their God—a return to his providential *presence*.

Now, because the symbol of God's presence among his people had historically been the temple built by Solomon in Jerusalem (1 Kings 9:3; 2 Kings 23:27; 2 Chronicles 20:9), and because God had warned the people that one significant result of their defection from the faith would be the destruction of Solomon's temple by foreign invaders (2 Chronicles 7:19–22), it's not surprising that the biblical story recounting the main events during the era of the return focused on rebuilding Solomon's temple and the city in which it was located (e.g., the Books of Ezra, Nehemiah, and Haggai).

According to the biblical saga, however, the Jews who had returned to the land quickly became distracted in their priorities and needed some divine encouragement to actually begin the rebuilding process. Thus, God graciously anointed the prophet Haggai to present these repatriated Jews with a message of both promise and indictment (Haggai 1:1–15). The promise portion of this prophetic utterance went like this:

> Then Haggai, the LORD's messenger, gave this message of the LORD to the people: "I am with you," declares the LORD. (Haggai 1:13)

Later, the same Jews experienced a profound sense of despair when the realization set in that the temple they had worked so hard to rebuild would lack the grandeur exuded by the previous one. Therefore God anointed the prophet Haggai to bring yet another divine word meant to encourage these weary workers (Haggai 2:1–9). At the heart of this second prophetic utterance, there likewise existed a promise of God's *presence*. Haggai 2:4 reads:

> "But now be strong, O Zerubbabel," declares the LORD. "Be strong, O Joshua son of Jehozadak, the high priest. Be strong, all you people of the land," declares the LORD, "and work. For I am with you," declares the LORD Almighty.

Haggai's contemporary during the postexilic era was the prophet Zechariah. We might wonder if Zechariah's prophetic work also reflected an emphasis upon God's presence. The answer is *Yes—and then some!* First of all, in his vision of Israel's future, Zechariah foretells a time when the people of Israel would be renowned for the simple but profound fact that God was *with* them:

> This is what the LORD Almighty says: "In those days ten men from all languages and nations will take firm hold of one Jew by the hem of his robe and say, 'Let us go with you, because we have heard that God is with you.'" (Zechariah 8:23)

Zechariah then speaks prophetically of the arrival of Israel's Messiah:

> "Rejoice greatly, O Daughter of Zion! Shout, Daughter of Jerusalem! See, your king comes to you, righteous and having salvation, gentle and riding on a donkey, on a colt, the foal of a donkey." (Zechariah 9:9)

In a sense, this is how the Old Testament portion of the biblical story of redemption ends: with a gracious promise of the eventual arrival of Israel's messianic king—a king whom the prophet Isaiah dubbed *Immanuel,* which means "God with us" (Isaiah 7:14; Matthew 1:23).

Thus, from all we've seen in this cursory study, it appears there really is biblical support for the idea that the experience of God's presence is at the heart of the Old Testament narrative as a whole. This, in turn, would seem to lend support for Woods' thesis that the spirituality of those living in the Old Testament era centered upon the idea of God being present to his people.

God's Presence as a Prominent Theme in the Psalms

Given what we've just discovered about the Old Testament biblical story, it shouldn't surprise us to discover that the Book of Psalms is replete with allusions to the possibility of experiencing God's presence, along with many exhortations to do so. It stands to reason that if the spirituality of the Old Testament centered on the idea of experiencing God, we would find references to this dynamic in the book that reflects Israel's prayers and songs of praise.[5]

Furthermore, the fact that the Bible's psalms speak so often of this spiritual experience helps to explain why, over the years, so many of Christianity's spiritual masters have extolled the virtues of the practice of the presence of God. The truth is that a systematic recitation of the Psalms has been a very important component in the spiritual formation pursued by monks, clerics, and lay Christians throughout the history of the Christian movement.[6]

Below is a concise treatment of many (not all) allusions to the presence of God that I have noted in reading the Psalms. I also include quotations of several relevant passages, many of which describe not only a particular way of experiencing God's presence but also the benefit of doing so. Again, my hope is that looking over these pertinent Scriptures, now and in the future, will serve as a source of inspiration with regard to the legitimacy and value of "the pursuit."

Allusions in the Psalms to the Possibility of Experiencing God's Presence

We begin by considering those portions of the biblical psalms that simply refer to the dynamic of being *with* God in a special, existential manner, as opposed to going through life without a sense of his presence and partnership. The Book of Psalms contains several passages that lament a sense of God's absence (see Psalm 10:1; 13:1; 27:9; 44:23–24; 69:17; 88:14; 102:2; 143:7) and a few others in which people—wicked people—actually celebrate what they perceive to be his absence (see Psalm 10:4; 14:1; 36:1; 53:1; 55:19; 94:1–7). The effect of both types of passages underscores the vital importance of the divine presence and encourages the reader to take full advantage of the wonderful possibility of *walking with God* rather than *going it alone.*

For example, in Psalm 14:4–5, we read that God is present in a special way among those who are sincerely devoted to him:

> Will evildoers never learn—those who devour my people as men eat bread and who do not call on the LORD? There they are, overwhelmed with dread, for God is present in the company of the righteous.

Because God is "present" among the righteous, the implication is that whatever the wicked do to the righteous, they do also to God! Passages such as this were intended, no doubt, to provide comfort for God's oppressed people.

Likewise, in Psalm 32:7 the psalmist refers to God as his "hiding place":

> You are my hiding place; you will protect me from trouble and surround me with songs of deliverance.

Evidently the psalmist knew that prayerfully entering into an experience of the presence of God made him feel more safe and secure than he otherwise would have felt.

Similarly, in several passages the psalmists refer to God as a "refuge," "fortress," and "shelter":

> God is our refuge and strength, an ever-present help in trouble. (Psalm 46:1)

> But I will sing of your strength, in the morning I will sing of your love; for you are my fortress, my refuge in times of trouble. (Psalm 59:16)

> He who dwells in the shelter of the Most High will rest in the shadow of the Almighty. I will say of the LORD, "He is my refuge and my fortress, my God, in whom I trust." (Psalm 91:1–2)

What can this kind of language mean except that the psalmists knew what it was to experience a sense of God's protecting presence?

This same idea shows up in other psalms in which the theme is the need for God's guidance and empowerment:

> Yet I am always with you; you hold me by my right hand. You guide me with your counsel, and afterward you will take me into glory. (Psalm 73:23–24)

> The LORD is with me; I will not be afraid. What can man do to me? The LORD is with me; he is my helper. I will look in triumph on my enemies. (Psalm 118:6–7)

How good to know that God is available to us as a source of divine guidance and enablement in the rough and tumble of life!

Given how important God's empowering presence was to David, it's no wonder that in Psalm 51:11–12 a repentant David pleads with

God not to withdraw his presence, following David's notorious sins involving Bathsheba and Uriah:

> Do not cast me from your presence or take your Holy Spirit from me. Restore to me the joy of your salvation and grant me a willing spirit, to sustain me.

Likewise, in several psalms, the psalmist begs God not to *hide his face*. For example, in Psalm 27:9 we read:

> Do not hide your face from me, do not turn your servant away in anger; you have been my helper. Do not reject me or forsake me, O God my Savior.

Such passages seem to imply an otherwise constant gaze of God upon his people. Indeed, the idea of living within the constant gaze of God shows up in Psalm 121—a well-loved passage in which the psalmist speaks of God *watching* over his people *constantly:*

> I lift up my eyes to the hills—where does my help come from? My help comes from the LORD, the Maker of heaven and earth. He will not let your foot slip—he who watches over you will not slumber; indeed, he who watches over Israel will neither slumber nor sleep. The LORD watches over you—the LORD is your shade at your right hand; the sun will not harm you by day, nor the moon by night. The LORD will keep you from all harm—he will watch over your life; the LORD will watch over your coming and going both now and forevermore.

Similarly, using metaphors and similes, various other psalms speak reassuringly of God's ongoing presence in the lives of those who belong to him. As an example, consider Psalm 125, which uses a vivid geographical image to remind the reader that the Lord *surrounds* his people:

> Those who trust in the LORD are like Mount Zion, which cannot be shaken but endures forever. As the mountains

surround Jerusalem, so the LORD surrounds his people both now and forevermore. (Psalm 125:1–2)

Consider also Psalm 139:7–10, another especially well-known passage that speaks of *God's steadfast presence* in our lives:

> Where can I go from your Spirit? Where can I flee from your presence? If I go up to the heavens, you are there; if I make my bed in the depths, you are there. If I rise on the wings of the dawn, if I settle on the far side of the sea, even there your hand will guide me, your right hand will hold me fast.

Psalm 84:1–5 poignantly expresses the psalmist's desire to remain continually in the presence of God:

> How lovely is your dwelling place, O LORD Almighty! My soul yearns, even faints, for the courts of the LORD; my heart and my flesh cry out for the living God. Even the sparrow has found a home, and the swallow a nest for herself, where she may have her young—a place near your altar, O LORD Almighty, my King and my God. Blessed are those who dwell in your house; they are ever praising you. Blessed are those whose strength is in you, who have set their hearts on pilgrimage.

This last passage does more than speak to us of the possibility of experiencing God's presence; it also prompts us to ask ourselves a crucial question: To what degree is my heart *set on pilgrimage?* This question, in turn, produces another: Are there things I should be doing to enter into an experience of God's presence? Both of these important questions lead us to the next stage in this study of "the pursuit" in the Psalms.

Allusions in the Psalms to Various Ways God's Presence Might Be Practiced

We now consider those passages in the Book of Psalms in which the psalmist specifies some action he took in order to experience the goodness, bigness, and dependability of God in a special way. Many of these passages imply that the reader should follow the psalmist's lead by engaging in the same kind of spiritual exercises.[8]

First, we take note of those psalms that speak of the need for God's people to *seek* him. For example, in Psalm 63:1, the psalmist speaks of seeking God in an especially earnest, almost desperate manner:

> O God, you are my God, earnestly I seek you; my soul thirsts for you, my body longs for you, in a dry and weary land where there is no water.

This is one of many passages in the Psalms that suggests there is something we can and should do, if we want to experience God's presence. Though his presence is ubiquitous, God doesn't force himself upon us; we must *seek* him in order to find him (see Psalm 9:10; 10:4; 14:2; 24:6; 27:4, 8; 40:16; 105:4; 119:2)!

What forms might our seeking the Lord take? In Psalm 16:7–8, the psalmist speaks of the spiritual comfort that results from doing that which is necessary to *set God before him:*

> I will praise the Lord, who counsels me; even at night my heart instructs me. I have set the Lord always before me. Because he is at my right hand, I will not be shaken.

Have you ever wondered what the psalmist had in mind here? If you haven't, why not? Why are we able to blow through passages such as this without really thinking through what it would take for us to follow suit? *Is it possible that the action involved in setting God before us might look a lot like practicing the presence of God?*

Going forward, Psalm 25:1 relates the psalmist's intent to *lift up his soul* to God:

> To you, O LORD, I lift up my soul.

Was this the psalmist's way of saying that he intended to attune himself to a sense of God's presence? This is one of several places in the Psalms where we read of this prayerful, joy-producing action being taken (see also, for example, Psalm 86:4; 143:8).

Furthermore, in Psalm 25:15, the psalmist goes on to assert that his eyes are "ever on the LORD":

> My eyes are ever on the LORD, for only he will release my feet
> from the snare.

Is this yet another way of saying that the psalmist was engaged in a form of "the pursuit"? And can't we discern the same pursuit-oriented dynamic in Psalm 59:9, where the psalmist speaks of *watching* for God?

> O my Strength, I watch for you.

To be a bit more precise about what's involved in pursuing God's presence, in Psalm 63:6–8, the psalmist speaks of making it a point to "remember" God, to "think" often of him, and to "cling" to him:

> On my bed I remember you; I think of you through the
> watches of the night. Because you are my help, I sing in the
> shadow of your wings. My soul clings to you; your right hand
> upholds me.

Surely it's easy to see how Brother Lawrence would have recommended these actions.

In the same vein, several psalms have the psalmist *praising God* "at all times," "always," and "all day long":

> I will extol the LORD at all times; his praise will always be on
> my lips. (Psalm 34:1)

My tongue will speak of your righteousness and of your praises all day long. (Psalm 35:28)

In God we make our boast all day long, and we will praise your name forever. (Psalm 44:8)

Don't these three passages sound similar to the perpetual praise involved in practicing the presence of God?

And, finally, a favorite passage of mine, Psalm 89:15–16, reads:

Blessed are those who have learned to acclaim you, who walk in the light of your presence, O LORD. They rejoice in your name all day long; they exult in your righteousness.

This passage speaks explicitly of *walking in the light of God's presence*. It seems to imply that learning to "acclaim" God—rejoicing and exulting in him often throughout the day—is the key to doing so! Once again, reading this passage causes the literary work of more than one spiritual master to come to mind.

The intent of this chapter is to show that the Old Testament documents as a whole—the Law, the Prophets, and the Writings—do indeed refer to, and advocate for, the practice of the presence of God. To the degree we're looking for biblical support for the holy habit we're calling "the pursuit," the Old Testament doesn't disappoint.

Now we ask: What will we do with what we've learned? Will we follow the lead of the psalmists and take advantage of the offer of God's empowering presence, or will we choose to trust in ourselves and in our own strength?

In the chapter that follows, we turn our attention to the documents of the New Testament. Will they also bear witness to the value of the pursuit of Christ's empowering presence? Let's find out.

———— 5 ————

SUPPORT FOR "THE PURSUIT" IN THE NEW TESTAMENT SCRIPTURES

Throughout the history of the Christian movement, believers have engaged in "the pursuit." But were they biblically justified in doing so? This is the overarching question we're dealing with at this stage in our journey together. In the previous chapter, we established that the spirituality of the Old Testament saints focused on the dynamic of God's presence. OK, but what kind of spirituality is promoted by the authors of the books written by the first followers of Jesus? Can we discern in the pages of the New Testament not only a theological foundation for "the pursuit" but actual exhortations to engage in it as well?

Personally, I consider these questions important. As I indicated in the last chapter, I'm the kind of Christian who feels it's important to do my best to live my life under the authority of Scripture. As much as possible, I want my beliefs and actions to be biblically informed (see Acts 17:11). This is just as true when it comes to my approach to spirituality as with anything else. Maybe more so! Who of us wants to waste our time engaging in spiritual exercises that won't really enable us to achieve the spiritual transformation we're so eager to experience?

On the other hand, if we discover that the authors of the New Testament actually were inspired by the Holy Spirit to include in their writings exhortations to engage in "the pursuit," then it stands to reason that we can count on the Holy Spirit's help as we endeavor to take these exhortations seriously! We might even conclude that a sincere, daily engagement in "the pursuit" is not just a *nicety*, but a *necessity*—a crucial component of a biblically informed walk with Christ!

So, did the Holy Spirit inspire the New Testament authors to include in their writings exhortations for us to pursue the experience of God's presence in our daily lives through a special focus on the risen Christ? I'm convinced he did.

New Testament References to the Theme of God's Presence in General

The first bit of evidence supporting the thesis stated above takes the form of a simple survey, which I believe will reveal that the writings of the New Testament echo the Old Testament emphasis upon God's presence. To begin, in Acts 17:28, we "hear" Paul speaking to the Athenian philosophers of God's pervasive presence in the world as a whole:

> "For in him we live and move and have our being." As some of your own poets have said, "We are his offspring."

The author of Hebrews refers to God's persistent presence in the lives of his people in particular:

> Keep your lives free from the love of money and be content with what you have, because God has said, "Never will I leave you; never will I forsake you." (Hebrews 13:5)

Furthermore, in other New Testament passages, Spirit-inspired authors refer to the importance of experiencing, and staying connected to, God's life-giving presence. For example, in Philippians 4:4–7, the apostle Paul encourages his readers to stay engaged in prayer. In the process, Paul presents the Philippians with a powerful promise regarding God's peace-producing presence in their lives.

> Rejoice in the Lord always. I will say it again: Rejoice! Let your gentleness be evident to all. The Lord is near. Do not be anxious about anything, but in everything, by prayer and petition, with thanksgiving, present your requests to God. And the peace of God, which transcends all understanding, will guard your hearts and your minds in Christ Jesus.

In his second epistle to the Corinthian Christians, Paul exhorts his readers to resist the temptation to syncretize (blend) their Christian faith with the paganism to which they were previously devoted. In so doing, he reminds them that, as Christians, they possess a very special, intimate relationship with God—one that involves a ceaseless sense of his presence. Paul quotes or alludes to several Old Testament passages as he writes:

> Do not be yoked together with unbelievers. For what do righteousness and wickedness have in common? Or what fellowship can light have with darkness? What harmony is there between Christ and Belial? What does a believer have in common with an unbeliever? What agreement is there between the temple of God and idols? For we are the temple of the living God. As God has said: "I will live with them and walk among them, and I will be their God, and they will be my people."
>
> "Therefore come out from them and be separate, says the Lord. Touch no unclean thing, and I will receive you."

"I will be a Father to you, and you will be my sons and daughters, says the Lord Almighty." (2 Corinthians 6:14–18)

A similar focus on the special relationship Christians have with God can be found in Revelation 21:1–3, where we find an inspiring description of what life will be like in the age to come. According to this passage, what makes heaven "heaven" is the experience of God's life-giving presence.

> Then I saw a new heaven and a new earth, for the first heaven and the first earth had passed away, and there was no longer any sea. I saw the Holy City, the new Jerusalem, coming down out of heaven from God, prepared as a bride beautifully dressed for her husband. And I heard a loud voice from the throne saying, "Now the dwelling of God is with men, and he will live with them. They will be his people, and God himself will be with them and be their God."

And yet, as beautiful as this passage is, the New Testament certainly is not teaching that we Christians must await the arrival of the new age to experience God's blessed presence. No, instead, the possibility of *continually experiencing more and more of God's reality in our lives here and now* seems to be at the heart of this prayer offered by the apostle Paul for the Ephesian believers:

> I pray that out of his glorious riches he may strengthen you with power through his Spirit in your inner being, so that Christ may dwell in your hearts through faith. And I pray that you, being rooted and established in love, may have power, together with all the saints, to grasp how wide and long and high and deep is the love of Christ, and to know this love that surpasses knowledge—that you may be filled to the measure of all the fullness of God. (Ephesians 3:16–19)

Finally, as he concluded one of his letters to the church in Thessalonica, Paul offered a benediction that linked the Thessalonian

Christians' experience of existential peace with what appears to be an ongoing sense that Jesus, the "Lord of peace," was *with* them in some palpable manner:

> Now may the Lord of peace himself give you peace at all times and in every way. The Lord be with all of you. (2 Thessalonians 3:16)

Passages such as these seem to support the idea that the New Testament authors' approach to spirituality, like the approach promoted in the Old Testament, focused on the experience of God's presence in the lives of the faithful.

However, as noted in chapter two, the big difference between these two spiritualities lies in their respective understandings of the significance of Jesus of Nazareth. Indeed, Paul's prayer for the Ephesian believers, as well as the benediction he directed toward the Thessalonian Christians, makes clear just how crucial the person of Christ is to the New Testament believer's experience of God.

New Testament References to the Presence of Christ in Particular

Why is Jesus of Nazareth so important to New Testament spirituality? In a nutshell, Christians believe that *God is uniquely present and accessible to human beings through the person of Jesus Christ, the historical embodiment of the second person of the Trinity* (see John 1:14–18). Moreover, due to their belief in the essential deity of Jesus, the authors of the New Testament, I believe, included in their writings certain passages that encourage their readers to experience God in a particular manner: *through a special focus on Jesus Christ.*

To be more specific, I suggest that *when the apostle Paul wrote Colossians 3:1–4, he had in mind an ongoing, mystical-experiential communion with the risen Christ—a perpetual pursuit of Christ's empowering presence that is key to a "Colossians 3 kind of life."* As you recall, this pivotal passage reads:

> Since, then, you have been raised with Christ, set your hearts on things above, where Christ is seated at the right hand of God. Set your minds on things above, not on earthly things. For you died, and your life is now hidden with Christ in God. When Christ, who is your life, appears, then you also will appear with him in glory.

So what do you think? Is it possible that this enigmatic passage really does support the pursuit of Christ's empowering presence as described in the first three chapters of this book? The remainder of this chapter provides some exegetical support for this idea in particular.

"Come and see"—Jesus' Method of Making and Forming Disciples

In addition to possessing an intimate, interactive relationship with God that tremendously influenced his own speech and behaviors (e.g., see John 5:18–20, 30; 14:10), Jesus encouraged his followers to cultivate the same for themselves.[1] The most basic manner in which Jesus went about enabling this ability within the lives of his disciples was not only to talk about its possibility but also to model it for them. This is why Jesus didn't simply conduct seminars; he recruited people to be *with him* on an ongoing basis. So we read in the Gospel of John that the very first disciples were made as a result of their having accepted Jesus' invitation to spend a day in his presence (John 1:35–41). Furthermore, Mark's Gospel indicates that Jesus' training regimen for those he designated "apostles" required that they be "with him" in a way that other disciples weren't:

> Jesus went up on a mountainside and called to him those he wanted, and they came to him. He appointed

twelve—designating them apostles—that they might be with him and that he might send them out to preach and to have authority to drive out demons. (Mark 3:13–15)

Being *with* Jesus—an important aspect of our apprenticeship to him—is also underscored in the story that contrasts Martha and her sister Mary's different choices when Jesus spent time in their home. The incident, related in Luke 10:38–42, is so germane to the topic at hand that it warrants being cited in full:

As Jesus and his disciples were on their way, he came to a village where a woman named Martha opened her home to him. She had a sister called Mary, who sat at the Lord's feet listening to what he said. But Martha was distracted by all the preparations that had to be made. She came to him and asked, "Lord, don't you care that my sister has left me to do the work by myself? Tell her to help me!"

"Martha, Martha," the Lord answered, "you are worried and upset about many things, but only one thing is needed. Mary has chosen what is better, and it will not be taken away from her."

This passage certainly appears to lend support to the idea that Jesus felt it important for his followers to spend time in his presence, fine-tuning their understanding of who he was and what he was about. Though Jesus was in the business of changing lives, he didn't choose to accomplish this by writing books for people to read, though that technology was certainly available to him. No, when Jesus really wanted to change someone's life, he encouraged that person to spend time with him!

"I am . . ."—Jesus' Transcendental Message

The Gospels go on to teach that when people such as Mary made the quality decision to spend time *with* Jesus they soon discovered they were in the presence of someone truly remarkable and unique. In the Gospel of John, in particular, we find a series of passages that portray Jesus claiming to be "living water" (John 4:10), the "bread of life" (John 6:35, 48, 51), the "light of the world" (John 8:12; 9:5), and the "gate" that leads to eternal life (John 10:7, 9). All of these passages refer to Jesus as someone much greater than a wise, ethical teacher. They portray him as someone uniquely able to meet humanity's most basic existential and spiritual needs.

Are we to think that this transcendental message of Jesus was intended only for the ears of his contemporaries? Or did Jesus, as he described himself in these ways, envision future generations of believers also experiencing the truth of these bold claims through a real relationship with him? I believe the Gospels present us with ample evidence that Jesus did indeed envision just such a thing.

"I will be with you"—Jesus' Promises of a Post-Easter Presence

Jesus plainly indicated at various times in his public ministry that, even though his destiny was to be handed over to Gentiles to be put to death, his disciples could still expect a real (though evidently mystical) sense of his empowering presence as they engaged in ministry themselves. For example, in Matthew 18:19–20 we read:

> Again, I tell you that if two of you on earth agree about anything you ask for, it will be done for you by my Father in heaven. For where two or three come together in my name, there am I with them.

And in Matthew 28:19–20, we find this famous promise:

> Therefore go and make disciples of all nations, baptizing them in the name of the Father and of the Son and of the Holy Spirit, and teaching them to obey everything I have

commanded you. And surely I am with you always, to the very end of the age.

Especially when viewed in their respective literary contexts, these passages make it perfectly clear that Jesus saw himself as someone able to provide some needed moment-by-moment mentoring for his followers *even after his own time on earth was over.* It was due to Jesus' supreme confidence in this fact that we have the above promises of his perpetual presence—promises that have proved over the years profoundly meaningful to his followers.

"Another Counselor"—Jesus' Promise of the Spirit

So how would Jesus be able to relate in an intimate, interactive manner with each of his followers even after his death? The night Jesus was arrested, he made another astounding promise to his disciples: after his death and resurrection, he would send his Spirit to be with them.

> I will ask the Father, and he will give you another Counselor to be with you forever—the Spirit of truth. The world cannot accept him, because it neither sees him nor knows him. But you know him, for he lives with you and will be in you. I will not leave you as orphans; I will come to you. (John 14:16–18)

Now the "Spirit of truth" in this passage is obviously the Holy Spirit. In various places in the New Testament, the Holy Spirit is referred to in one way or another as Jesus' Spirit (see Romans 8:9; Galatians 4:6; Philippians 1:19; 1 Peter 1:11). So at the risk of oversimplifying, we can say that the reason why Jesus could promise to be available to provide his disciples with the moment-by-moment mentoring they would need to fulfill their own ministry assignments even after his time on earth was over was because he knew that once he had returned to his Father, his own Spirit would descend into their lives.

"If anyone opens the door"—The Concept of Christ Indwelling Our Hearts

John the Evangelist goes on to report that, after hearing Jesus make the amazing promise cited above (i.e., John 14:16–18) and a subsequent, similar promise (see John 14:21), one of Jesus' incredulous disciples asked why the Lord would reveal himself only to his followers and not to the world as a whole. In response, Jesus made yet another promise that further supports the argument made in this chapter:

> Jesus replied, "If anyone loves me, he will obey my teaching. My Father will love him, and we will come to him and make our home with him." (John 14:23)

This idea of the resurrected and ascended Jesus somehow making his home with each of his disciples is reminiscent of another famous passage found in the writings of the apostle John. In Revelation 3:20, the risen Christ states:

> Here I am! I stand at the door and knock. If anyone hears my voice and opens the door, I will come in and eat with him, and he with me.

As we've already seen in Ephesians 3:17, Paul speaks of Christ *dwelling in our hearts* through faith. Thus, even though the Bible doesn't actually speak of the need for people to "invite Jesus into their hearts," it's easy to see where the idea came from. The concept of Jesus somehow residing at the right hand of the Father while also being *at home* in the lives of his followers is very much supported in the biblical text. Wouldn't this suggest that the authors of the New Testament had in mind some sort of ongoing, mystical-experiential communion with the risen Christ?

"Abide in me"—Jesus' Call for Us to Remain Connected

At the same time, the New Testament makes it clear that such a spiritual communion with Christ needs to be maintained, lest it be lost or rendered impotent. For example, I believe John 15:1–8 can be interpreted in a way that encourages us to engage in "the pursuit":

> I am the true vine, and my Father is the gardener. He cuts off every branch in me that bears no fruit, while every branch that does bear fruit he prunes so that it will be even more fruitful. You are already clean because of the word I have spoken to you. Remain in me, and I will remain in you. No branch can bear fruit by itself; it must remain in the vine. Neither can you bear fruit unless you remain in me.
>
> I am the vine; you are the branches. If a man remains in me and I in him, he will bear much fruit; apart from me you can do nothing. If anyone does not remain in me, he is like a branch that is thrown away and withers; such branches are picked up, thrown into the fire and burned. If you remain in me and my words remain in you, ask whatever you wish, and it will be given you. This is to my Father's glory, that you bear much fruit, showing yourselves to be my disciples.

Yes, I'm aware that this passage can be interpreted simply as a call for Jesus' disciples to remain faithful to him and his teachings—to never defect from their commitment to his lordship or even allow themselves to be distracted in their discipleship. We might refer to this as a *volitional-intellectual* connection with Christ. Interpreted in this way, the passage need not imply an ongoing *mystical-experiential* communion with the risen Jesus after all.

Then again, why must we choose between these two interpretive options, as if Jesus' intention in this famous exhortation had to be one or the other? As important as it is for us to remain diligent volitionally in our study of Christ's teachings (i.e., his "words"), isn't it also necessary for us to experience an ongoing sense of his spiritual presence in our lives? Doesn't the larger context of this passage (John 14–17) argue for a both/and, rather than an either/or, interpretation of this powerful passage?

I would make the same argument with regard to another New Testament passage that can be interpreted in either a volitional-intellectual or mystical-experiential manner. In Galatians 2:20, the apostle Paul boldly states:

> I have been crucified with Christ and I no longer live, but Christ lives in me. The life I live in the body, I live by faith in the Son of God, who loved me and gave himself for me.

Of course it's possible to interpret this passage, with its reference to Christ living within Paul, in a manner that's entirely metaphorical and not in any sense literal. According to this interpretation, Paul was only insisting that his hope of salvation rested solely upon his faith in the cross-work of Christ, not in any futile attempt on his part to keep the law of Moses. According to this reading of Galatians 2:20, Paul was simply indicating his commitment to maintain a volitional-intellectual connection to Christ.

Surely we shouldn't miss this point. It is important to reject a legalistic approach to the Christian faith and to hold tightly to the message of grace. But once again, why must we choose between the two methods of interpretation—metaphorical and literal—and the two types of connectedness to Christ that they yield—volitional-intellectual and mystical-experiential? Isn't it at least possible that Paul might *also* have thought of the Spirit of Jesus actually residing within him, enabling and empowering him to live his life for the one who had died for him? Indeed, I'm convinced that a careful reading of related passages (such as Romans 6:1–14 and 2 Corinthians 5:14–21) indicates that the apostle Paul believed that a dynamic, interactive relationship existed between a literal experience of the risen

Christ in our lives and our ability to live for him! *According to Paul, it's vitally important that we maintain both a volitional-intellectual and a mystical-experiential relationship with Jesus!*

"I am Jesus, whom you are persecuting" —The Risen Christ in the Book of Acts

The fact is that the Book of Acts provides powerful portrayals of the kind of ministry fruitfulness that does indeed occur when Jesus' disciples stay connected to him in a manner that is mystical-experiential as well as volitional-intellectual. As a whole, this document records for us how Christ's first followers, filled with his Spirit, proceeded to turn the world on its ear in his name (see Acts 17:6)! However, when we drill a bit more deeply into the text, we find that Luke describes not only the things that Christ's Spirit empowered his disciples to say and do (e.g., Acts 4:8–13, 31; 8:39; 9:31; 10:9–23; 13:2, 9–12) but also the things that were accomplished by "the Lord" himself (e.g., Acts 2:46–47; 11:21; 14:3; 16:14), the things that were accomplished on behalf of Christ via the agency of an angel (e.g., Acts 5:17–20; 8:26; 10:3–8; 12:7–11; 27:23–26), and finally those times when, in an apparently mystical manner, *Jesus himself* showed up alongside someone in need of a personal word of admonition, encouragement, or ministry guidance (see Acts 7:55–56; 9:3–6, 10–17; 18:9–10; 22:17–21; 23:11).

Talk about an ongoing experience of intimate interactivity with the risen Christ! Truly, we need look no further than the Book of Acts to be convinced that the possibility of such a relationship possesses biblical warrant. Even so, our analysis of the New Testament's support for the pursuit of Christ's empowering presence is not yet complete.

"Fix your eyes (and thoughts) on Jesus"
—Apostolic Advice for Being Formed in Christ

Even a cursory reading of the letters sent by the apostles to the various New Testament churches reveals how concerned these authors were to encourage their readers to maintain both a volitional-intellectual and a mystical-experiential connection to Christ. In broad strokes, the apostolic advice with regard to both endeavors was for Christ-followers such as you and me to stay centered spiritually by *continually attuning ourselves to Jesus.*

In some passages, New Testament authors come right out and call for their readers to *fix their eyes (or thoughts) on Jesus.* For example, it was apparently the concern of the unnamed author of the Epistle to the Hebrews to encourage his Jewish Christian readers to maintain their commitment to Christ, despite the sociopolitical pressure they were experiencing to back away from him. Toward this end, the writer penned the following passages:

> Therefore, holy brothers, who share in the heavenly calling, fix your thoughts on Jesus, the apostle and high priest whom we confess. (Hebrews 3:1)

> Therefore, since we are surrounded by such a great cloud of witnesses, let us throw off everything that hinders and the sin that so easily entangles, and let us run with perseverance the race marked out for us. Let us fix our eyes on Jesus, the author and perfecter of our faith, who for the joy set before him endured the cross, scorning its shame, and sat down at the right hand of the throne of God. Consider him who endured such opposition from sinful men, so that you will not grow weary and lose heart. (Hebrews 12:1–3)

These passages seem to teach that, by staying focused on Jesus, his followers can experience over and over again the inspiration required to finish the race, remaining faithful to their heavenly calling. And lest we conclude this focus was merely a volitional-intellectual exercise in which the believer occasionally recalls the example of commitment provided by the historical Jesus, other passages written by the same author emphasize the ongoing activity of the risen Christ in the daily lives of his followers (e.g., see Hebrews 4:14–16).

Another way in which the apostolic authors advised their readers to attune themselves to Jesus was by exhorting them to *clothe themselves with Christ*. Paul refers to this spiritual exercise in his letter to the Christians in Rome. In the process, he suggests that a connection exists between clothing ourselves with the Lord Jesus Christ and the experience of moral transformation.

> The night is nearly over; the day is almost here. So let us put aside the deeds of darkness and put on the armor of light. Let us behave decently, as in the daytime, not in orgies and drunkenness, not in sexual immorality and debauchery, not in dissension and jealousy. Rather, clothe yourselves with the Lord Jesus Christ, and do not think about how to gratify the desires of the sinful nature. (Romans 13:12–14)

According to this passage, the alternative to Christians clothing themselves with Christ is continuing the old habit of *thinking about how to gratify the desires of the sinful nature*. When we pay attention to this fact, it becomes apparent that Paul was calling his readers to position themselves to experience a moral transformation—by developing the new habit of *focusing their thinking on the person of Jesus*. This connection between the experience of moral transformation and the dynamic of one's thinking focused on Christ seems to have been a staple in the apostle Paul's arsenal of pastoral counsel. Using slightly different language, he offers essentially the same advice in passages such as Romans 6:1–14, Romans 8:5, 2 Corinthians 11:3, Ephesians 4:21–24, and, as will be discussed later at length, Colossians 3:1–4.[2]

Simply put, it appears that the apostles of Jesus routinely taught Christians in their day that the key to experiencing moral and spiritual formation in Christ was to take control of their thought life, making a deliberate effort to focus their thinking on Jesus.

But does this necessarily require a mystical-experiential connection with Christ? Good question!

"You have been raised with Christ" —A Very Basic Christian Concept

All that we've learned so far in this chapter brings us back around to that pivotal Pauline passage that reads:

> Since, then, you have been raised with Christ, set your hearts on things above, where Christ is seated at the right hand of God. Set your minds on things above, not on earthly things. For you died, and your life is now hidden with Christ in God. When Christ, who is your life, appears, then you also will appear with him in glory. (Colossians 3:1–4)

Ironically, this enigmatic, hard-to-interpret passage actually presents to us a concept that is very basic to the Christian life: *a mystical union does indeed exist between the resurrected and ascended Jesus and his earthbound disciples, and our ongoing recognition of this mystical union makes it possible for us to actually become like the one we say we're following.* Let's take a closer look at how this works.

I've already made a passing reference to Romans 6:1–14, where the apostle Paul clearly identifies the key to the Christian disciple's ability to replace old, sinful habits of living with new, righteous ones: *recognize* and *count on* the fact that a mystical but real relationship exists between the baptized believer and the risen Christ. *According to this profoundly important passage, our identification with the death and resurrection of Jesus makes it possible for fully devoted Christ-followers to die to sin and begin living a new kind of life for God here and now.* The key to Christian sanctification, says Paul, is to keep this important reality in mind and to live our lives daily based on it! Here's the heart of what Paul says in this crucial text:

Don't you know that all of us who were baptized into Christ Jesus were baptized into his death? We were therefore buried with him through baptism into death in order that, just as Christ was raised from the dead through the glory of the Father, we too may live a new life.

If we have been united with him like this in his death, we will certainly also be united with him in his resurrection. For we know that our old self was crucified with him so that the body of sin might be done away with, that we should no longer be slaves to sin—because anyone who has died has been freed from sin. Now if we died with Christ, we believe that we will also live with him. For we know that since Christ was raised from the dead, he cannot die again; death no longer has mastery over him. The death he died, he died to sin once for all; but the life he lives, he lives to God.

In the same way, count yourselves dead to sin but alive to God in Christ Jesus. (Romans 6:3–11)

Paul certainly seems to be speaking here of a spiritual, experiential connection between the risen Christ and his earthbound disciples, a mystical union Paul also refers to in Romans 8:11, Ephesians 1:3, and possibly in Galatians 2:20. Keep all of this in mind as we turn our attention back to Colossians 3:1–4, which provides fairly explicit support for our engagement in the pursuit of Christ's empowering presence.

✠ Colossians 3:1–4—The Historical and Literary Context

Most biblical commentators agree that a heretical teaching, which mandated an adherence to certain religious rules and rituals and advocated some kind of devotion to angelic beings, had infiltrated the church in Colosse. It threatened to cause the disciples there to become disconnected to Christ, the head of the church (Colossians

2:16–19). Alarmed at this disturbing development, Paul's ultimate message to this confused and beleaguered community of faith was *to stay focused on, rooted in, and connected to Christ* (see Colossians 2:1–12).

In the process of encouraging the Colossian Christians to continue *living in Christ* (Colossians 2:6), Paul offered a cogent critique of the heretical teaching to which they were being exposed. He pointed out its powerlessness to do the very thing its proponents had promised: help them overcome their human bent toward sensual indulgence (Colossians 2:20–23).

Immediately after pointing out the complete inability of this false gospel to help its adherents experience any sort of genuine moral transformation, Paul offered his readers the pastoral counsel found in Colossians 3:1–4. At the risk of oversimplifying things, I suggest that this very basic counsel called for the Colossian Christians to do two simple things: (a) recognize the mystical union that exists between themselves and the risen Christ, and (b) develop the habit of focusing their hearts and minds (affections and thinking) on things above, "where Christ is" (i.e., on the risen Christ himself).

Paul then followed this very basic pastoral counsel with a vivid description of the lifestyle those who take him seriously will most certainly be able to achieve (Colossians 3:5–17). In a nutshell, *the apostle Paul indicates that those who follow his counsel will develop the ability to become new beings, whose every word and action reflect the mentoring influence of the one in whom the fullness of divine wisdom and knowledge, and deity itself, dwells* (Colossians 3:17; see also Colossians 2:3, 9).

Colossians 3:1–17—The Implications

What does all this mean? Among other things, it means that the apostle Paul encouraged his readers to maintain their volitional-intellectual connection to the historical Jesus by being careful to maintain a mystical-experiential connection to the risen Christ! Or, to put it simply, it means there really is cause to believe that in Colossians 3:1–4 Paul had in mind something akin to what I refer to as "the pursuit."

Stop and think about it. Can you think of a better way to forge a "Colossians 3 kind of life"? How else, besides a daily engagement in the spiritual exercise that is the chief topic of this book, are we to fulfill the ethical imperatives put before us in Colossians 3:5–17? Once again, I boldly suggest that a sincere, daily engagement in "the pursuit" is not just a *nicety,* but a *necessity*—a crucial component of a biblically informed walk with Christ! This spiritual exercise is anything but a waste of time, and we most certainly can count on the Holy Spirit's help as we attempt to practice it!

My goal in the last two chapters has been to help you recognize that there is indeed biblical support for a sincere engagement in the pursuit of Christ's empowering presence. In the next couple of chapters we explore in depth a related idea: according to Christianity's spiritual masters, an intention to maintain a moment-by-moment mentoring relationship with Jesus is the key to becoming the kind of Christ-follower whose words and actions really do reflect his influence. Is this truly your desire? Well then, turn the page and allow our journey together to continue.

SUPPORT FOR "THE PURSUIT" IN THE CORPUS OF DEVOTIONAL LITERATURE

Dallas Willard opened the "Spirituality and Ministry" seminar I attended in the summer of 2002 by stating one of his goals for that postgraduate course: when those of us participating in the seminar left the retreat center after two weeks, we would never again be in a hurry! Hearing this, I couldn't help but raise one eyebrow and sneak a look around the room to see if any of the other seminar participants shared my sense of incredulity. *Surely I didn't just hear him say that an earmark of genuine Christian spirituality is the absence of busyness in our lives!* In the course of the seminar, I discovered that Willard wasn't suggesting that we ministers would come to the place where we stopped being *busy*. He *was* indicating, however, the possibility that we could experience an interactive intimacy with Jesus that would keep us, despite our busyness, from being *hurried* as well.

Since I tend to suffer from what John Ortberg refers to as the "hurry sickness," I was intrigued.[1] You might even say that I was hooked. As Willard began encouraging this group of ministers to make it their intention to take their spirituality more seriously, the first thing he did was speak to us of a practical benefit that such a choice would yield in our daily lives.

This motivational approach is one nearly all the spiritual masters take in their writings. Scattered throughout the corpus of devotional literature are some glowing descriptions of the benefits that inevitably result from practicing the presence of God. Like the more general references to this holy activity presented in chapters 1 through 3, these additional, even more enthusiastic accounts can be quite compelling.

Thus, in this simple, no-nonsense chapter, we survey what some of Christianity's spiritual masters have said about the many *benefits* we can expect to experience as we endeavor each day to pursue Christ's empowering presence. My desire is that this discussion of the practical benefits will further encourage you to make it your intention to do whatever is necessary to begin seriously engaging in this crucial spiritual exercise. And my hope, once again, is that the collection of quotes presented in the following pages will serve as an *oasis of inspiration* to which you can return for spiritual refreshment any time you find yourself experiencing a dry season in your spiritual journey.

Brother Lawrence

We begin this survey, as we did the one presented in the first section of this book, with a look at the venerable Brother Lawrence. This time, however, our focus is on what this godly monk had to say about the spiritual value of cultivating an ongoing conversation with God. Presented below are some of the benefits of "the pursuit," derived from Brother Lawrence's conversations and writings.

✠ The pursuit of Christ's empowering presence is a source of great joy.

In their evangelistic encounters with others, many Christians refer to the wonderful sense of joy a commitment to Christ produces within a believer's heart. Perhaps we would do better to speak of the *potential* for such joy, since it's obvious that many of us, the truth be known, tend to allow this benefit of the faith to slip through our fingers! On the other hand, it seems Brother Lawrence believed he knew the secret of experiencing real Christian joy in this life.

> I have quitted all forms of devotion and set prayers but those to which my state obliges me. And I make it my business only to persevere in His holy presence, wherein I keep myself by a simple attention, and a general fond regard to God, which I may call an *actual presence* of God; or, to speak better, an habitual, silent, and secret conversation of the soul with God, which often causes me joys and raptures inwardly, and sometimes also outwardly, so great that I am forced to use means to moderate them and prevent their appearance to others.[2]

✠ The pursuit of Christ's empowering presence enables us to effectively deal with the devil.

Like Jesus, Peter, and Paul, Brother Lawrence took the devil seriously. Do you? Do you routinely remember it's never just you and God and your circumstances, and that you have a real spiritual enemy whose goal is to drive a wedge between you and God and everything God offers? Echoing the spiritual warfare counsel provided by James 4:7, Brother Lawrence offers some warfare counsel of his own:

> We must go about our labors quietly, calmly, and lovingly, entreating Him to prosper the works of our hands; by thus keeping heart and mind fixed on God, we shall bruise the head of the evil one, and beat down his weapons to the ground.[3]

✠ **The pursuit of Christ's empowering presence represents the most appropriate act of worship we can offer a gracious God.**

In Romans 12:1–2, the apostle Paul exhorts his readers, on the basis of the wonderful gift of grace God bestowed upon them, to recognize that a reasonable response of worship calls for them to do much more than strive to obey a few rules and engage in an assortment of religious rituals. Instead, they should eagerly offer their very selves to God as living sacrifices. Presumably, Paul had in mind the idea of their voluntarily becoming enslaved to the will of a good God in the way they lived their lives. In other words, everything they were and had was to be devoted to God.

The two passages below—in which Brother Lawrence argues for the propriety of pausing periodically throughout each day to interact with God—remind me of Romans 12:1–2. See what you think. The good brother writes:

> Since you cannot but know that God is with you in all you undertake, that He is at the very depth and centre of your soul, why should you not thus pause an instant from time to time in your outward business, and even in the act of prayer, to worship Him within your soul, to praise Him, to entreat His aid, to offer Him the service of your heart, and give Him thanks for all His loving-kindnesses and tender-mercies?
>
> What offering is there more acceptable to God than thus throughout the day to quit the things of outward sense, and to withdraw to worship Him with the secret places of the soul?[4]

> In very truth we can render to God no greater or more signal proofs of our trust and faithfulness, than by thus turning from things created to find our joy, though for a single moment, in the Creator.[5]

Thomas à Kempis

Though in this survey we draw only a single quote from *The Imitation of Christ,* the pursuit-produced benefit derived from this sole citation is extremely important.

> ✠ **The pursuit of Christ's empowering presence can make the difference between a heart that's hardened and disconsolate and one that's filled with comfort and delight.**

Surely all of us have gone through seasons during which our spiritual eyes weren't as focused on Christ as they could have been. What usually occurs during these spells of distracted discipleship is that we lose a sense of God's life-giving involvement in our lives. What if a key to breaking such a spell or ending such a season was making a renewed commitment to pursue Christ's empowering presence throughout our days? Wouldn't that be a valuable discovery? I believe support for this very notion can be found in the following citation in which à Kempis exhorts his readers to prioritize "the pursuit":

> When Jesus is with us, all is well, and nothing seems hard; but when Jesus is absent, everything is difficult. When Jesus does not speak to the heart, all other comfort is unavailing; but if Jesus speaks but a single word, we are greatly comforted. . . . Oh, happy the hour when Jesus calls us from tears to joy of spirit! How arid and hard of heart you are without Jesus! How foolish and empty if you desire anything but Jesus! Surely, this is a greater injury to you than the loss of the whole world.[6]

Frank Laubach

I perceive in Laubach's writings on spirituality something of an innocent, schoolboy fascination with the prospect of maintaining an ongoing sense of God's presence in his life. His descriptions of experiences with "the pursuit" effuse a sort of giddy delight, which, in turn, makes reading these descriptions a delightful experience. As you look over the benefits listed below, I trust you'll soon see what I mean.

✠ The pursuit of Christ's empowering presence provides us with a remarkable sense of divine help in the present and hope for the future.

Athletes sometimes speak of finding themselves "in the zone," a place in which it seems that time slows, their focus sharpens, muscles cooperate with acute precision, and the "bounces" in the game keep coming their way as if by divine fiat. This experience of being "in the zone," they say, explains their ability to turn in "peak performances."

From time to time I've also experienced being in the zone, both athletically and spiritually in my walk with Christ. Perhaps you have too. Spiritually speaking, sometimes it seems we're able to spend a whole day "in the zone." When this happens, everything just falls into place as we go about our duties. Living in a Colossians 3 manner actually seems doable, as we're acutely aware of God's providential presence all day long! This kind of zone experience is, I believe, something akin to that which Laubach had in mind when he wrote:

> I feel simply carried along each hour, doing my part in a plan which is far beyond myself. This sense of cooperation with God in little things is what so astonishes me, for I never have felt it this way before. I need something, and turn around to find it waiting for me. I must work, to be sure, but there is God working along with me. To know this gives a sense of security and assurance for the future which is also new to my life. I seem to have to make sure of only one thing now,

and every other thing "takes care of itself," or I prefer to say what is more true, God takes care of all the rest. My part is to live this hour in continuous inner conversation with God and in perfect responsiveness to His will. To make this hour gloriously rich. This seems to be all I need think about.[7]

✠ The pursuit of Christ's empowering presence produces within us a new feeling of cleanness before God and disgust for everything unholy.

Fairly often, college students come to me for counseling, confessing not only their inability to conquer sin in their lives but also admitting that, deep inside, they don't really want to stop doing what they know is wrong. Let's be honest, haven't we all been in this position? Is there any help for us—any reason to believe that we might someday come to the place where our moral values line up more closely with God's? Frank Laubach would say there is. Suggesting that a commitment to engage in "the pursuit" will have a transformative effect upon the condition of our hearts, Laubach writes:

> I have tasted a thrill in fellowship with God which has made anything discordant with God disgusting. This afternoon the possession of God has caught me up with such sheer joy that I thought I never had known anything like it. God was so close and so amazingly lovely that I felt like melting all over with a strange blissful contentment. Having had this experience, which comes to me now several times a week, the thrill of filth repels me, for I know its power to drag me from God. And after an hour of close friendship with God my soul feels clean, as new fallen snow.[8]

✠ The pursuit of the empowering presence of Christ produces within us a single-minded focus that

improves our psychology, health, appearance, and the performance of our day-to-day activities.

I referred above to Laubach's schoolboy fascination with "the pursuit." I recently looked up the meaning of the word "ingénue," discovering that it refers to a naïve girl or young woman. Obviously, Frank Laubach doesn't qualify as an ingénue. And yet, there really is a sense of giddy delight that's discernible in the manner in which he extols the virtues of the practice of God's presence. According to the following quote, engaging in this holy exercise will dramatically improve just about every area of our lives, including our appearance!

> As I analyze myself I find several things happening to me as a result of these two months of strenuous effort to keep God in mind every minute. This concentration upon God is strenuous, but everything else has ceased to be so. I think more clearly, I forget less frequently. Things which I did with a strain before, I now do easily and with no effort whatever. I worry about nothing, and lose no sleep. I walk on air a good part of the time. Even the mirror reveals a new light in my eyes and face. I no longer feel in a hurry about anything. Everything goes right. Each minute I meet calmly as though it were not important. Nothing can go wrong except one thing. That is that God might slip from my mind if I do not keep on my guard. If He is there, the universe is with me. My task is simple and clear.[9]

A. W. Tozer

One of the courses I teach nearly every semester at a Christian liberal arts university is entitled "Foundations of the Christian Life." This freshman-level course is designed to encourage all incoming students, regardless of their major, to begin their postsecondary educational experience thinking about the need to integrate their Christian faith (at whatever level it exists) with their learning and living, and to provide them with the skills to do so. As part of this course, my students read Tozer's *The Pursuit of God*. This Christian classic is written in a sermonic manner—a literary style completely unfamiliar to many of my students. Nevertheless, each semester it's not uncommon for students to send me e-mails indicating that their experience with Tozer was genuinely life altering. I'm convinced that a big reason for Tozer's appeal lies in the fact that he encourages his readers to engage in "the pursuit," suggesting that doing so is crucial to the Christian life in a couple of ways:

✠ The pursuit of Christ's empowering presence enables us to achieve the sanctification that even college students hunger for deep inside!

Like Laubach, Tozer encourages us to believe that an ongoing sense of Christ's real presence in our lives can't help but improve our ability to say no to sin and yes to righteousness. He seems to believe that focusing on Christ, instead of on ourselves, is the key to experiencing an empowering, sanctifying grace from God.

> The man who has struggled to purify himself and has had nothing but repeated failures will experience real relief when he stops tinkering with his soul and looks away to the perfect One. While he looks at Christ the very things he has so long been trying to do will be getting done within him. It will be God working in him to will and to do.[10]

✠ The pursuit of Christ's empowering presence takes us to a new level in our walk with God.

Many say that members of the emerging generations possess a special craving for authenticity. Then again, don't we all—no matter how old we are or how long we've been in "the Way" (see Acts 24:14)—want to believe there's more to the Christian life than what we've experienced thus far? I'm convinced that, deep inside, most of us who name the name of Christ are still holding on to the hope that we will someday experience the kind of dynamic Christian living reflected in the pages of the New Testament. This appears to be the very passion that Tozer aims to stir within his readers.

> When the habit of inwardly gazing Godward becomes fixed within us we shall be ushered onto a new level of spiritual life more in keeping with the promises of God and the mood of the New Testament. The Triune God will be our dwelling place even while our feet walk the low road of simple duty here among men. We will have found life's *summum bonum* indeed.[11]

Leslie Weatherhead

One benefit present in the writings of many spiritual masters is the lofty idea that pursuing Christ's empowering presence enables us to achieve the *summum bonum* ("supreme good") of life. I suggest that the idea originated with the apostle Paul. After he prescribed "the pursuit" in Colossians 3:1–4, he immediately describes the lifestyle and calls his readers to make sure that everything they say and do is effected "in the name of the Lord Jesus, giving thanks to God the Father through him" (Colossians 3:17). I don't know how anyone could articulate a more comprehensive moral imperative than this! And yet, Paul seemed to believe that engaging in "the pursuit" could make this existentially fulfilling way to live possible.

We've already seen other spiritual masters, such as Tozer, echo Paul on this point. And before our journey together is complete, we'll come across others. In fact, next on the list of such "echoers" is Leslie Weatherhead, whose writing reminds us of the following benefit.

✤ The pursuit of Christ's empowering presence eventually leads to the sanctifying of every part of life—and, thus, to the end of our spiritual wanderings.

Indeed, in the poignant quote presented below, we find that as Weatherhead alludes to the sanctifying effect of "the pursuit," he suggests that the privilege of experiencing this perfecting "friendship" with Jesus is the very thing we were made for—the final destination of every human being's spiritual search. A huge claim, don't you think? Weatherhead writes:

> It is an amazing offer. It means that no single experience of life has ever to be faced alone. What would it mean to us if in the temptation to hasty temper, to meanness, contempt, jealousy, impurity, avarice, we could pull ourselves up with the thought that this patient, kind, but inexorable Friend was near? What would it mean in sorrow, in bereavement, in pain, in loneliness? What would it mean in joy and laughter, in pleasure and fun? It would mean the sanctifying of every part of life. It is the experience our fathers called "being saved," for to be received into this friendship is to be at the end, not indeed of our journey but of all fruitless wanderings.[12]

Richard Foster

I've already acknowledged my own tendency to allow legitimate busyness to cause me to adopt a hurried, harried approach to life.

Giving in to the perception that I need to hurry in order to accomplish everything that needs to be done in a day usually causes me to become impatient with myself, my circumstances, and other people (especially those who threaten to interrupt or add to my agenda). Therefore, it may be due to my own issues that I resonate so strongly with Richard Foster's depiction of yet another primary benefit of "the pursuit." Here's how I would articulate this pursuit-produced blessing:

✠ **The pursuit of Christ's empowering presence enables us to possess a new Center of Reference that, in turn, injects a valuable sense of peace and serenity into our otherwise harried and hurried lives.**

In the following quote, Foster seems to anticipate that all of his readers will relate to the simple but profound spiritual problem described above. Is this true of you? If so, then perhaps Foster's reassuring words will be as refreshing to you as they are to me. Speaking of the possibility of finding, through the exercise of unceasing prayer, a solid, steady existential "center" for our lives, Foster writes:

> I am sure you sense the desperate need for Unceasing Prayer in our day. We pant through an endless series of activities with scattered minds and noisy hearts. We feel strained, hurried, breathless. Thoughts dart in and out of our minds with no rhyme or reason. Seldom can we focus on a single thing for long. Everything and anything interrupt our sense of concentration. We are distracted people.
>
> Unceasing Prayer has a way of speaking peace to chaos. We begin experiencing something of the cosmic patience of God. Our fractured and fragmented activities begin focusing around a new Center of Reference. We experience peace, stillness, serenity, firmness of life orientation.[13]

Dallas Willard

No one I know describes the benefits of "the pursuit" with as much precision, and in such a compelling manner, as Dallas Willard. The winsome nature of Willard's writings on spiritual formation may be due to his own success at having mastered the masters, learning from them in the process. It may also flow from the tremendous sense of personal conviction with which he treats the theme of being formed in Christ. Whatever the reason, I find it incredibly easy to take Willard at his word as he clearly suggests that engaging daily in the "hot pursuit of Christ" will most certainly *transform one's whole life!*

This is one of the main messages I take away from Willard's groundbreaking book, *Renovation of the Heart: Putting on the Character of Christ.* Due to Willard's direct and significant influence upon my own thinking with regard to "the pursuit," I will analyze his treatment of the effects of Christ's empowering presence in a bit more detail. Furthermore, a by-product of the following cursory treatment of Willard's approach to spiritual formation will be additional support for the two main arguments I make in this book: (a) "the pursuit" is the key to experiencing a "Colossians 3 kind of life," and (b) this particular spiritual exercise is at the heart of Christian spirituality.

Willard: On the Need for Spiritual Formation in General

According to Willard, if history tells us anything, it tells us that the greatest need of every human being is a renovation of the heart.[14] On the one hand, Willard speaks of an age-old and worldwide spiritual quest—a quest that is rooted in "the deep personal and even biological need for goodness that haunts humanity."[15] On the other hand, Willard observes that "societies the world around are currently in desperate straits trying to produce people who are merely capable of coping with their life on earth in a nondestructive manner."[16]

Too many people in our world live in ways that detract from, rather than contribute to, human flourishing. Too many people routinely engage in behaviors that end up harming themselves and others. This is anything but the way God intended that human beings created in his image should live. Deep in our hearts, we know this is true.

The problem is that humanity, like Humpty Dumpty, has experienced a great "fall" and is in desperate need of being made right again. Willard states, "The greatest need you and I have—the greatest need of collective humanity—is *renovation of our heart*. That spiritual place within us from which outlook, choices, and actions come has been formed by a world away from God. Now it must be transformed."[17] Thus Willard contends that there exists everywhere in our fallen world a profound need for human beings to be re-formed at the core of their being in such a way as to make them whole again, able to live as God originally intended.

Willard: On the Nature of Spiritual Formation in General

Another way to understand Willard's call for a renovation of the heart is as an invitation for individuals to become more intentional regarding their *spiritual formation*. Willard explains that in a most basic sense spiritual formation "is the process by which the human spirit or will is given a definite 'form' or character."[18] As such, Willard points out that spiritual formation is something everyone experiences—in one direction or another.

> The most despicable as well as the most admirable of persons have had a spiritual formation. Terrorists as well as saints are the outcome of spiritual formation. Their spirits or hearts have been formed. Period.
>
> We each become a certain kind of person in the depths of our being, gaining a specific type of character. And that is the outcome of a process of spiritual formation as understood in general human terms that apply to everyone, whether they

want it or not. Fortunate or blessed are those who are able to find or are given a path of life that will form their spirit and inner world in a way that is truly strong and good and directed Godward.[19]

So the question is not whether we will experience a spiritual formation, but rather what direction our spiritual formation will take us and how involved we will be in the process.

Willard: On the Direction of Christian Spiritual Formation in Particular

For Christians, says Willard, the intended direction of spiritual formation is nothing other than the very character of Christ. Hence Willard's statement that "spiritual formation for the Christian basically refers to the Spirit-driven process of forming the inner world of the human self in such a way that it becomes like the inner being of Christ himself."[20]

As we've already seen, Willard is famous for saying that fully formed Christ-followers are those who live their lives the way Jesus would if he were they.[21] We're talking about a profound change from the inside out, not from the outside in. Describing those who've made progress along the path of Christian spiritual formation, Willard is careful to state:

> Now, these people are not perfect and do not live in a perfect world—yet. But they are remarkably different. The difference is not one of a pose they strike, either from time to time or constantly, or of things they do or don't do—though their behavior too is very different and distinctive. Where the children of light differ is primarily and most importantly on the "inside" of their life. It lies in what they are in their depths.[22]

My primary mentor is suggesting that it's actually possible to come to the place where we want what Christ wants, value what

Christ values, do what Christ would do if he were living our life. Does this bold assertion pique your interest as it does mine? Wouldn't it be nice to believe that the result of engaging in "the pursuit" is a profound change at the core of our being, not simply an acquired ability to maintain a more pious persona?

Willard explains that this is what Jesus has always been about. Jesus' agenda to bring a rebellious world back under the dominion of its creator is not by means of "the formation of social institutions and laws," but through a "revolution of *character* which proceeds by changing people from the inside through *ongoing personal relationship to God in Christ* and to one another."[23] As human beings are transformed at their core, the social structures they create will likewise experience transformation, toward being more just and humane, in line with God's original intention (see Micah 6:8).[24]

Willard: On the Process of Christian Spiritual Formation

So how, according to Willard, does this inner transformation actually occur? The first thing that must be underscored is that transformation, while involving human effort, can never be achieved by mere human means alone.

> The instrumentalities of Christian spiritual formation therefore involve much more than human effort and actions under our control. Well-informed human effort certainly is indispensable, for spiritual formation is no passive process. But Christlikeness of the inner being is not a human attainment. It is, finally, a gift of grace.
>
> Though we must act, the resources for spiritual formation extend far beyond the human. They come from *the interactive presence of the Holy Spirit* in the lives of those who place their confidence in Christ. They also come from the spiritual treasures—people, events, traditions, teachings—stored in the body of Christ's people on earth, past and present.[25]

Willard goes on to stipulate, "Grace does not rule out method, nor method grace. Grace thrives on method and method on grace."[26] In other words, it's due to God's goodness that a path toward recovering the kind of life we were created to live is even possible. The great desire of God's Spirit is to supernaturally form Christ in the lives of those who make the quality decision to walk that path. At the same time, whether or not we travel the road that leads to Christlikeness is a question all of us must answer for ourselves. God won't force the experience of Christian spiritual formation on anyone who doesn't desire it or who won't take the steps necessary to experience it!

Next, we must remember Willard's contention that there are "six basic aspects in our lives as individual human beings"[27] and that the ideal of the spiritual life is one where all the essential parts of the human self (thought, feeling, choice, body, social context, and soul) are effectively *organized around God*.[28] In a nutshell, for Christian spiritual formation to occur within us, we simply must take seriously the goal of becoming God-focused, God-intoxicated human beings.[29]

OK, so how does that happen? How does one become "intoxicated" with God? What actual activities are involved? In a sense, the entirety of *Renovation of the Heart* is an answer to this question. Therefore, I realize that I'm greatly oversimplifying a very detailed, comprehensive discussion of spiritual formation when I make the following two suggestions. First, I suggest that we think in terms of God having provided us with many spiritual disciplines that, when engaged in for the right reasons and in the right way, *can* bring us face-to-face, so to speak, with Christ's empowering, transforming presence.

My second suggestion is that we embrace the idea that the *ultimate* goal of engaging in any spiritual discipline—whether it be prayer, fasting, study, worship, service, solitude, silence, celebration, or others—is to increase our ability to experience Christ's empowering presence throughout our days. Embracing this idea will have the effect of informing (a) what we expect to result from our engagement in the disciplines, (b) the manner in which we practice the disciplines, and (c) the way in which we measure how successful our spiritual exercises have been.

Does Willard offer any support in *Renovation of the Heart* for the idea that engaging in "the pursuit" is as critical to one's spiritual formation as I'm suggesting? I believe he does.

First, we've already noted that, in many places within his work, Willard makes abundantly clear his conviction that the key to (or at least the starting point for) seeing our lives effectively organized around God lies in our thought life. It's crucial, Willard says, that the apprentice of Jesus develops the habit of *continually thinking about God,* and does so rightly! When our minds are filled with accurate thoughts of God, a new, empowering worldview is created—a new, God-informed perspective on our existence that will produce within us new godly attitudes and, as a result, new godly actions. (I'll say more about this in the next section.)

Second, Willard at least implies that *the role of the various spiritual disciplines is to help us become more Christ-focused in our thinking.*

> There are certain tried-and-true disciplines we can use to aid in the transformation of our thought life toward the mind of Christ. Disciplines are activities that *are* in our power and that enable us to do what we cannot do by direct effort. We cannot transform our ideas and images, or even information we have or our thought processes, into Christlikeness by direct effort. But we can do things—adopt certain practices—that, indirectly, will increasingly have that effect.[30]

Disciplines that help us transform our thought life toward the mind of Christ. Is this really possible? Willard is convinced that it is. Evidently believing that it's vitally important for his readers to be likewise convinced, he writes:

Hopefully, it will now be clear that our inner (and therefore outer) being can be transformed to increasingly take on the character of Christ. That transformation is not only *possible,* but has *actually* occurred to a significant degree in the lives of many human beings; and it is *necessary* if our life as a whole is to manifest his goodness and power, and if we as individuals are to grow into the eternal calling that God places upon each life.[31]

This is precisely what I mean when asserting that the pursuit of Christ's empowering presence is at the heart of Christian spirituality! Furthermore, all that has been said thus far about the need, nature, direction, and process of Christian spiritual formation leads naturally to the final section of this chapter, which discusses the benefits of "the pursuit."

Willard: On the Result of Christian Spiritual Formation

Having already seen that Willard is convinced that it's possible for Christ's followers to become transformed into his very image, we are now in a position to formally state that Willard's writing on Christian spirituality seems to suggest the following:

> ✠ **The pursuit of Christ's empowering presence is the key to organizing our thoughts, feelings, choices, body, social context, and soul around God, thus becoming the kind of people whose lifestyles begin to do justice to Colossians 3:5–17.**

Though to my knowledge Willard never uses the phrase "Colossians 3 kind of life," I can attest to the fact that he has his students memorize Colossians 3:1–17 in order to meditate often upon this key passage as they cultivate their spirituality. I'm convinced that Willard would agree that this portion of Scripture is remarkable in its ability to encapsulate the goal of a healthy engagement in Christian spiritual formation. A big reason for this confidence is the quote presented below. Please note how this extremely compelling citation from Willard's work begins with an indirect reference to "the pursuit," then indicates how an ongoing sense of God's presence in our lives will influence our thoughts, our attitudes, and ultimately our actions.

> The effect of standing before God by welcoming him before us will, by contrast, be the transformation of our entire life. All else that enters our mind, and especially the thoughts that first come to mind as we encounter various kinds of events that make up our lives, will be healthy, godly, and those in harmony with the realities of a good-God-governed universe, not the illusions of a godless or a me-governed universe, or one where man is supreme—or no one else. My patterns of thinking will conform to the truths of scriptural revelation, and I will extend and apply those truths, under the guidance of God's Holy Spirit, to all of the details of my daily life.
>
> Am I undertaking some task? Then I in faith do it with God, assuming and finding his power to be involved with me. That is the nature of his kingdom. Is there an emergency? I meet it with the knowledge that God is in the midst of it with me and will be calm in a center of intense prayer. Am I praised? My thoughts (and feelings) will move immediately to the goodness of God in my life. Am I condemned or reproached? I know that God is supporting and helping me because he loves me and has a future for me. Am I disappointed and frustrated? I rest in the knowledge that God is over all and that he is working things out—that "all things work *together* for good to those who love God and are called into the fulfillment of his purposes." And so forth.[32]

Wouldn't it be great to actually live like this? Doesn't this sound amazingly reminiscent of a "Colossians 3 kind of life"?[33]

I hope this description of the life of a spiritually mature Christ-follower resonates within our hearts and rises up as a volitional force to create within us the level of *intention* (steadfast resolve) necessary to learn to practice the presence of God. Remember, God's grace doesn't make our engagement in "the pursuit" unnecessary; it's what makes it possible. We all must make our own decision to become God-focused, God-intoxicated people! *Have you done this yet?*

I began part two of this book with a quote from Richard Foster in which he encourages us to come home to God's presence. Hopefully, the material presented in the last three chapters has successfully caused you to want to continue with me on this journey.

Coming home to God's presence sounds great—but how do we get there? It's time to enter the final phase of the trek we're taking together. Keep reading. The final chapters of this work provide some specific steps all of us can take toward a more Christ-focused life . . . and our spiritual home.

PART THREE

MEANS:

How We Might Proceed in The Pursuit of Christ's Empowering Presence

---

7

JEREMY TAYLOR'S STRATEGY FOR PRACTICING "THE PURSUIT"

Early one morning I was meditating on Mark 14:66–72, which relates the story of Peter disowning Jesus on the night of his arrest. Here's how the passage concludes: "Immediately the rooster crowed the second time. Then Peter remembered the word Jesus had spoken to him: 'Before the rooster crows twice you will disown me three times.' And he broke down and wept" (Mark 14:72).

As I closed my Bible and reached to take another sip of coffee, I thought of the words, "Then Peter remembered the word Jesus had spoken to him," and wondered, *What if Peter had remembered Jesus' word of warning during his interactions with those by the fire, rather than afterward? What if Peter had experienced a sense of Christ's presence throughout the entire incident?*

I'm pretty sure this would have made a huge difference in the big fisherman's performance during that awful evening. And though the New Testament would lack a poignant story that imparts some vital lessons regarding the weakness of the flesh on the one hand, and the depth of God's grace on the other (see Mark 16:7), Peter himself would have been spared the horrible spiritual agony he surely experienced for the next seventy-two hours or so of his life. The bottom line is that, as we saw in the previous chapter, the habit of continually communing with Christ's empowering presence really can dramatically affect the way we live!

So how do we do it? What's actually involved in a daily engagement of this spiritual exercise that has received so much attention by so many spiritual masters throughout the history of the Christian movement? These are the questions the final two chapters of this book will attempt to answer.

In his book *Holy Living*, seventeenth-century Anglican churchman Jeremy Taylor not only references the spiritual practice I've been describing, but he also puts forward a set of "rules" designed to enable his readers to experience the presence of God and respond appropriately to it. As the title of Taylor's book suggests, his focus was on *holy* living. The goal of this chapter is to familiarize ourselves with Taylor's ten rules (or guidelines) for cultivating a *sanctifying* sense of God's presence in our lives.

I begin this survey of Taylor's ten rules by issuing several important caveats. First, Taylor's approach to the phenomenon of God's presence can come off as a bit austere, perhaps even puritanical, especially when compared to the romance and friendship rhetoric we've seen other spiritual masters use when referring to the same dynamic. This explains why I began this chapter with a reflection on the story of Peter's defection from the faith, with its awful immediate consequences.

As we survey Taylor's prescriptions related to practicing God's presence, it's imperative that we keep in mind this pastor's overarching goal: *to help his readers sin less.* This particular pastoral objective flavors the nature of the discussion. That is, some of Taylor's "rules" seem to be as much about *why* we should honor God's presence (the fear of the Lord) as they are about *how* we should do so. And yet, even though Taylor was not at all averse to sternly reminding his readers to reverence and respect the holy God in whose presence they continually dwelt, Taylor's aim was also to encourage his readers, in his own way, to love and appreciate this God.

Second, writing during the Elizabethan era in English history, Taylor was known in his day as the "Shakespeare of the pulpit."[1] Thus the prose he employs may seem, by our standards, somewhat antiquated and at times difficult to comprehend. (Then again, Shakespeare is not always easy to understand the first time around, right?) Even so, what this devout chaplain and pastor has to say about holy living is true and sensible and can serve as a solid foundation for our discussion of ways we may cultivate the experience of Christ's empowering presence. So, I encourage you to take the time to read—and reread when necessary—the powerful quotes presented in this chapter, prayerfully pondering their significance for your spiritual journey. My hope is that a careful reading of Taylor will yield rich rewards in terms of both information and inspiration.

With these two caveats in place, let's look at Taylor's ten rules (guidelines) for holy living. I begin each rule with a brief introduction designed to help us better ascertain Taylor's meaning; my conclusion is intended to help us apply the rule to our lives.

Rule #1

Taylor begins the spiritual counsel he offers in *Holy Living* by exhorting his readers to meditate often on one theological attribute in particular: God's omnipresence. In other words, we need to keep reminding ourselves that God is everywhere around us. Though Taylor chose to reference Psalm 139 toward this end, he might have also cited Acts 17:28, where the apostle Paul reminds his Athenian audience that it's in God that we live and move and have our very being. The idea in both biblical passages is that we simply can't escape

God; his presence is constantly pressing in upon us, just waiting to be experienced by us. Taylor argues that an ongoing mindfulness of this fact will surely cause us to take God seriously and make us passionate about pleasing him in everything we do.

> Let this actual thought often return, that God is omnipresent, filling every place; and say with David, "Whither shall I go from Thy spirit, or whither shall I flee from Thy presence? If I ascend up into heaven, Thou art there . . ." (Psalm 139:7, 8). This thought by being frequent will make an habitual dread and reverence towards God, and fear, in all actions. For it is a great necessity and engagement to do unblameably when we act before the Judge who is infallible in His sentence, all-knowing in His information, severe in His anger, powerful in His providence, and intolerable in His wrath and indignation.[2]

Taylor's rhetoric is definitely more somber than that of other spiritual masters. And yet, what the English divine says here is true, isn't it? Doesn't the Epistle to the Hebrews present the same essential message? "Nothing in all creation is hidden from God's sight. Everything is uncovered and laid bare before the eyes of him to whom we must give account" (Hebrews 4:13).

Perhaps Taylor's stern spiritual counsel to cultivate an ongoing sense of reverence and respect for the holy God "with whom we have to do" (the KJV rendering of Hebrews 4:13) is precisely what we need, since we live in an increasingly post-Christian, morally relativistic cultural environment.

Rule #2

Taylor's second "rule" has to do with the way in which his readers conduct their times of devotion. Taylor suggests we begin our quiet times by spending a few moments in worship: picturing God with the eyes of faith; rehearsing why he is worthy of our time, attention, and praise; imagining ourselves in his very presence. According to Taylor, this simple act of connecting with God in a way that is both volitional-intellectual and mystical-experiential will have a tremendously positive effect upon our devotional exercises.

> In the beginning of actions of religion, make an act of adoration, that is, solemnly worship God, and place thyself in God's presence, and behold Him with the eye of faith; and let thy desires actually fix on Him as the object of thy worship, and the reason of thy hope, and the fountain of thy blessing. For when thou hast placed thyself before Him and kneelest in His presence, it is most likely all the following parts of thy devotion will be answerable to the wisdom of such an apprehension, and the glory of such a presence.[3]

When talking to my university students in class or in one-to-one counseling sessions, I often make the distinction between conversing *with* God and merely talking *at* him. What some of us are really doing during "prayer" is merely rehearsing our worrisome thoughts *toward the idea of God,* rather than genuinely sharing our burdens with him in a real, person-to-person manner.

I'm convinced that Jesus would have us understand that prayer can be a real conversation with God, confident that we're being listened to by a gracious, loving heavenly Father who genuinely cares for us. This kind of praying produces (a) a real sense of peace in our hearts, and (b) real results in the world! *Rather than merely talk at, or worry toward, the idea of God, we can and should converse with him.* To do this, we need to take rule #2 seriously and begin our prayer times with an act of adoration, reckoning with God's real presence, focusing our heart and mind on the fact that we are about to converse with a very real spiritual entity who also happens to be our loving heavenly Father.[4]

Rule #3

Taylor goes on to point out that meditating on the attributes of God shouldn't be something we do only during our quiet times. Instead, we should cultivate the habit of allowing each experience we have in the course of a day to remind us of some attribute or characteristic of God.

> Let everything you see represent to your spirit the presence, the excellency, and the power of God; and let your conversation with the creatures lead you unto the Creator; for so shall your actions be done more frequently with an actual eye to God's presence, by your often seeing Him in the glass of creation. In the face of the sun you may see God's beauty; in the fire you may feel His heat warming; in the water, His gentleness refresh you: He it is that comforts your spirit when you have taken cordials; it is the dew of heaven that makes your field give you bread, and the breasts of God are the bottles that minister drink to your necessities. This philosophy, which is obvious to every man's experience, is a good advantage to our piety; and by this act of understanding our wills are checked from violence and misdemeanor.[5]

What if we were to develop the habit of allowing everything we see, and everyone we speak with, to remind us of some wonderful, life-sustaining, life-enhancing attribute of God? Taylor's take is that every aspect of creation is ultimately a divinely caused miracle that in one way or another reflects the Creator's goodness, bigness, and dependability. With some effort we can grow in our ability to "see" and "enjoy" God in all our daily experiences.

Don't be too quick to dismiss this exercise as unrealistic. First, with some practice you may be surprised at how good you can become at it. Second, it may be that living a truly God-intoxicated life requires that we take a spiritual formation "rule" such as this seriously!

Rule #4

We saw in the previous guideline that Taylor's focus seemed to shift from being careful to fear God to being careful to appreciate him. We're about to find that there's a softer feel to rule #4 as well. Here Taylor encourages his readers to *build within their hearts a chapel* in which God may be adored all day long, despite their busy schedules. In other words, Taylor exhorts us in this next quote to develop the habit of communing with God throughout each day of our lives—from the time we rise in the morning to the time we go to bed at night, and during every activity in between.

> In your retirement, make frequent colloquies or short dis-coursings between God and thy own soul. "Seven times a day do I praise Thee; and in the night season also I thought upon Thee while I was waking." So did David; and every act of complaint or thanksgiving, every act of rejoicing or of mourning, every petition and every return of the heart in these intercourses, is a going to God, an appearing in His presence, and a representing Him present to thy spirit and to thy necessity. And this was long since by a spiritual person called, "a building to God a chapel in our heart." It reconciles Martha's employment with Mary's devotion, charity and religion, the necessities of our calling and the employments of devotion. For thus in the midst of the works of your trade you may retire into your chapel, your heart; and converse with God by frequent addresses and returns.[6]

It's true that in 1 Thessalonians 5:17 the apostle Paul directs his readers to "pray continually." But whenever I hear Christians as-sert, on the basis of this passage, that they prefer to pray throughout the day rather than limit their prayer time to the morning hours, I'm tempted to wonder if they really pray throughout the day or if this is just an excuse for not engaging in a daily devotional routine. Personally, I don't think it has to be an either-or proposition. I'm

CHRIST'S EMPOWERING PRESENCE

convinced that a morning devotional routine that's conducted properly greatly aids my ability to "obey" both rule #3 and #4 and thus 1 Thessalonians 5:17. Yes, I should retreat often each day into the chapel in my heart to pray, but it appears that this heart-chapel must be reconstructed each morning!

Can you relate at all to what I'm saying? Are you careful to begin each day rebuilding the heart-chapel into which you can retire often to commune with Christ?

Rule #5

In his fifth rule, Taylor explicitly calls for a balance between fear and love in our response to God's continual presence in our lives. In the process, Taylor puts forward the idea that God is at work in "every accident of our lives." In other words, Taylor says we can and should see God in every event that takes place during the day and, no matter what the occurrence, continually look to God and ask questions such as "Lord, what are you up to?" and "How would you have me respond to this?"

> Represent and offer to God acts of love and fear; which are the proper effects of this apprehension, and the proper exercise of this consideration. For as God is every where [sic] present by His power, He calls for reverence and godly fear: as He is present to thee in all thy needs, and relieves them, He deserves thy love: and since in every accident of our lives we find one or other of these apparent, and in most things we see both, it is a proper and proportionate return that to every such demonstration of God we express ourselves sensible of it by admiring the divine goodness, or trembling at His presence; ever obeying Him because we love Him, and ever obeying Him because we fear to offend Him. This is that which Enoch did, who thus "walked with God."[7]

—— 142 ——

So here is Taylor's formula: because God is at work in every situation either to confront or to comfort us, we should be careful all day long to obey his promptings and/or to offer thanks for his gifts. Can this be accomplished in a way that avoids our becoming superspiritual? I believe it can. I'm convinced that it's possible to do all this in a demure manner that avoids giving those around us the impression that we're continually "on the phone" with God!

Rule #6

Rule #6 calls for us to recognize that our relationship with God truly is *interactive* in the sense that God's dealings with us are to some degree a genuine *response* to the way we live before him. We need to remember the biblically supported concept that grace makes obeying and cooperating with God's work in our lives possible, not unnecessary. Taylor writes:

> Let us remember that God is in us, and that we are in Him: we are His workmanship, let us not deface it; we are in His presence, let us not pollute it by unholy and impure actions. God hath "also wrought all our works in us" (Isaiah 26:12); and because He rejoices in His own works, if we defile them and make them unpleasant to Him, we walk perversely with God and He will walk crookedly towards us.[8]

Taylor speaks here of the possibility of our walking "perversely with God" and his walking "crookedly towards us." One way to understand what Taylor is saying in this cryptic quote is this: God will, for our sake, sometimes choose not to reveal himself to us if we've developed the habit of being careless in our words and deeds or if we harbor known sin in our hearts. God is under no obligation to richly reveal himself in a transformational manner if we are deliberately engaging in gross hypocrisy (see 1 John 3:6). It's one thing to be sincere, but as yet imperfect; it's another to intentionally live a double life! Thus, it's been the experience of many Christians (including me) that God will sometimes withdraw his presence for a season in order to get our attention and incite within us a renewed desire to be pleasing to him (see Psalm 51:11–12; Ephesians 4:26–32). The bottom line is that if we want to experience Christ's empowering presence fully, then we simply must be careful to avoid walking perversely with him.

Rule #7

In his seventh rule, Taylor reminds us of the biblical teaching that what we do to our brothers and sisters in Christ we also do to God (see Proverbs 19:17; Matthew 25:40). Located as it is among his ten rules for practicing God's presence, I'm inclined to interpret Taylor as teaching that God is pleased to reveal himself in an especially powerful way to those who minister comfort to the poor and hurting and seek justice for the oppressed. He writes:

> God is in the bowels of thy brother; refresh them when he needs it, and then you give your alms in the presence of God, and to God; and He feels the relief which thou providest for thy brother.[9]

What would happen if a multitude of Christ's followers—eager to experience his empowering presence (or because they've had such an experience[10])—were to begin acting in accordance with Taylor's seventh rule, providing refreshment to those in need around them? I believe that a fresh sense of divine presence would invade the lives of not only those engaged in "the pursuit" but also the recipients of these grace-inspired acts of kindness. Could this be what Jesus had in mind when he encouraged his disciples to function as light and salt in a world filled with darkness and decay (Matthew 5:13–16)?

Rule #8

One of the biggest criticisms offered by many non-Christians in our day is that too many churchgoers act one way in church on Sunday but a completely different way the rest of the week. Way ahead of his time, Taylor addresses this lamentable dynamic in his eighth rule, which calls us to make it our goal to live every moment of every day as if we were in a church service—in the very presence of God and his gathered people.

> God is in every place: suppose it therefore to be a church; and that decency of deportment and piety of carriage which you are taught by religion, or by custom, or by civility and public manners, to use in churches, the same use in all places: with this difference only, that in churches let your deportment be religious in external forms and circumstances also; but there and every where [*sic*], let it be religious in abstaining from spiritual undecencies, and in readiness to do good actions: that it may not be said of us, as God once complained of His people, "Why hath My beloved done wickedness in My house?" (Jeremiah 11:15).[11]

Again, Taylor seems to suggest that because our relationship with God is personal, he really can be disappointed and even grieved by our willful misbehavior. Evidently, one reason "the pursuit" has a transformative effect upon those who take it seriously is that the promise of his presence is conditioned upon our willingness to take seriously the idea of being in a truly intimate, interactive relationship with him. It's a dialectic: experiencing Christ's presence empowers us to be holy; a commitment to be holy allows us to experience his presence more fully and profoundly. This is one of many paradoxes we find in the Scriptures.

Rule #9

As I write these words I'm flying back to Southern California from Minneapolis, where I presented a scholarly paper at an academic conference. During one of the plenary sessions, one scholar read a paper arguing that Christ didn't die just for human beings, but for all of creation as well. He concluded his presentation with these words: "So if you don't think that Jesus died for your dog as well as for you, your theology needs to be readjusted!"

Though he doesn't go quite this far, Taylor's ninth rule does suggest that another way we can grieve God, and in some way fail to experience his presence, is to be cruel to any of his creatures (see Proverbs 12:10).

> God is in every creature: be cruel towards none, neither abuse any by intemperance; remember that the creatures, and every member of thy own body, is one of the lesser cabinets and receptacles of God; they are such which God hath blessed with His presence, hallowed by His touch, and separated from unholy use by making them to belong to His dwelling.[12]

I admit to being less than certain about all that Taylor had in mind in this guideline. Frankly, I suppose it's possible that the animal abuse Taylor had in mind was sexual in nature. At the very least, Taylor seems to say there's a connection between our experience of God's presence and the need to avoid being *abusive or cruel* to our pets, our livestock, perhaps even the snail crossing the trail upon which we're hiking. Could it be that every time we take pains not to be cruel to one of God's creatures we are reminded of our creator's loving concern for us? After all, we're creatures too!

Rule #10

If Taylor's ninth rule is a bit enigmatic, his tenth rule is anything but! In an obvious, straightforward manner, the English divine instructs us to learn to *talk to God about everything and to do so with complete honesty*. According to Taylor, there's absolutely nothing we can't bring before God. Furthermore, we need to get it in our heads that we can and should be completely honest with God, even about our doubts. The bottom line is that going to God in prayer should be something we do all day long, every day of our lives—our first response, not our last resort. Taylor describes in the following quote that kind of lifestyle:

> He walks as in the presence of God that converses with Him in frequent prayer and frequent communion; that runs to Him in all his necessities, that asks counsel of Him in all his doubtings; that opens all his wants to Him; that weeps before Him for his sins; that asks remedy and support for his weakness; that fears Him as a judge, reverences Him as a lord, obeys Him as a father, and loves Him as a patron.[13]

What a fitting way for Taylor to conclude his ten rules. This exhortation appears to strike a balance in the how and the why of our practice of God's presence. I want to draw special attention to Taylor's insistence that a part of "the pursuit" involves the habit of asking God for "remedy and support" for our weaknesses. In other words, when we mess up (and we will!), we are to acknowledge our failure, simply and honestly, and beseech God for more empowerment to do better in the future. Here is grace. Certainly we should strive to reverence and obey God, doing our very best not to offend or grieve him. But when (not if) we do manage to disappoint, we can and should go to him, asking for his forgiveness and spiritual assistance.

Surely Taylor had Psalm 51 in mind as he wrote this final rule, especially verses 10 through 12, which read:

> Create in me a pure heart, O God, and renew a steadfast spirit within me. Do not cast me from your presence or take your

Holy Spirit from me. Restore to me the joy of your salvation and grant me a willing spirit, to sustain me.

Now that's an inspiring quote to keep nearby!

The goal of this chapter is to make you aware of the ten "rules" for practicing the presence of God that the seventeenth-century Anglican churchman, Jeremy Taylor, included in his book *Holy Living*. I suggested from the outset that the focus of Taylor's approach to "the pursuit" was the sanctifying effect it can have in the lives of those who engage in it. Taylor was obviously concerned that Christ's followers learn to live holy lives before a holy God.

Now lest this approach strike us as too austere and "old-fashioned" to be of value to us, we should continually keep in mind the story of Peter's denial of Jesus and the horrible sense of shame and guilt he experienced as a result. It was because Jesus was so very real to the big fisherman that his act of betrayal toward his Lord grieved him so. This begs the question: Do contemporary Christ-followers fully recognize how our sinful acts of disobedience grieve the heart of our loving heavenly Father? Does the knowledge that we've grieved God cause us to mourn the way Peter did (see Mark 14:72 and Matthew 5:4)? If not, why? If so, then maybe what Taylor said about how to experience and respond appropriately to God's continual presence is something we need to heed after all.

In the final two chapters, I provide other practical suggestions for how you can engage in the pursuit of Christ's empowering presence. If you're like me, you're probably thinking that you can use all the help you can get! Fortunately for all of us, even more help is on the way.

——— 8 ———

HOW VARIOUS SPIRITUAL LIFE AUTHORS SUGGEST WE ENGAGE IN "THE PURSUIT"

Are you feeling a bit overwhelmed at the prospect of cultivating a vibrant Christian spirituality? There's no need. Dominican theologian Simon Tugwell states, "So long as we imagine that it is we who have to look for God, we must often lose heart. But it is the other way about; he is looking for us."[1] In a similar vein, Jan Johnson reminds us,

> We cannot accomplish the habit of enjoying God's presence; God accomplishes it in us. "We easily forget that [praying] is a supernatural act which is therefore beyond our own strength and can only be performed by the inspiration and help of grace," wrote Jean Nicholas Grou. "We must earnestly ask God to produce it in us, and then we must perform it tranquilly under his guidance." Instead of fussing, striving, and monitoring, we surrender ourselves to God over and over again. For those of us who are hooked on productivity, this approach is radical.[2]

As a person who tends to be hooked on productivity, I like that Johnson, citing Grou, encourages us to engage in "the pursuit" in a manner that is tranquil rather than strained, trusting God to help us as we earnestly surrender ourselves to him. I also appreciate Tugwell's encouragement for us to never lose heart, always remembering that Christ's quest for us predates and underwrites our pursuit of him.

I've written elsewhere of the great need for evangelical Christians to recognize and deal with the Pharisaical attitudes and actions that occur all too frequently among us.[3] One of the actions often associated with Pharisaism is religious legalism—the idea that one's right standing before God is achieved by strict adherence to a set of religious laws. As we continue our survey of some specific suggestions for engaging in the pursuit of Christ's empowering presence, I exhort us to avoid turning "the pursuit" into some sort of spiritual work or viewing it as an onerous burden that must be borne if we are to "stay on God's good side."

Why this concern? For one thing, I'm afraid that anyone reading the previous chapter might be tempted to adopt Jeremy Taylor's "rules" of holy living in a legalistic manner, as if right standing before God is something we must achieve and maintain through our own hard work. No, "the pursuit" should be viewed as an approach to Christian spirituality that is grace-oriented through and through. It is not only made possible by grace, but when engaged in properly, it produces gracious people!

Second, despite using the word "should" in this chapter as I articulate more ways Christ's empowering presence might be pursued, this word choice is not meant to imply that we are guilty of sin if we don't employ each and every one of these specific suggestions. What follows is thoughtful, field-tested advice on how we *might* increase our ability to maintain an ongoing communion with Christ, not a list of hard-and-fast religious rules that all of us must live by or else!

On the other hand, we must do something! In *The Life You've Always Wanted,* John Ortberg writes:

> How do we go about transforming ordinary, fallen hearts into hearts that love the right thing in the right way to the right degree with the right kind of love? It requires a plan of action; otherwise it will never happen. William Paulsell advises us, "It is unlikely that we will deepen our relationship with God in a *casual* or *haphazard manner.* There will be a need for some intentional commitment and some reorganization in our own lives. But there is nothing that will enrich our lives more than a deeper and clearer perception of *God's presence in the routine of daily living.*"
>
> The CEO of a Fortune 500 company would never try to grow an organization without some strategic planning. A coach serious about winning would never enter a season in a "casual or haphazard manner." We understand the need for wise, flexible planning in other important matters such as finances. The need is just as great in pursuing spiritual life.[4]

Ortberg makes the point that while spiritual transformation can't be completely controlled by us, neither will it occur if it's left to chance. The history of Christian spirituality, including that modeled for us by Jesus, indicates that healthy spirituality needs some structure—a set of spiritual exercises engaged in fairly regularly—as well as the ability to be flexibly responsive to the unpredictable workings of the Spirit. Ortberg suggests that we think of this structure as a sort of trellis supporting the vine that is our spiritual life in the Lord.[5] He goes on to explain:

> Historically, when Christians sought to order the events of ordinary life around growing in Christlikeness, they would develop what is called a "rule of life." Various monastic orders each had a rule. This was not simply a set of laws. The Latin word for rule is *regula*—that is, something done regularly.

A rule involves a rhythm for living in which we can grow more intimately connected to God. In particular, finding a strategy for transformation will involve questions such as:

- How and when will I pray?
- How will I handle money in a way that draws me closer to God?
- How can I approach work in a way that will help Christ to be formed in me?
- How am I involved in Christian community (such as corporate worship, fellowship, and confession)?
- How can I fill my daily tasks with a sense of the presence of God?[6]

This chapter is about assisting you in building a support structure, in creating a "rule of life"—that is, helping you decide what activities you will use on a frequent, perhaps daily basis to increase your experience of Christ's empowering presence. The following pursuit-oriented strategies, put forward by various spiritual life authors (mostly contemporary), have been most impactful in my life and can be helpful to you as well.

I present these various suggestions with a minimum of editorial commentary—just enough to get us thinking a bit more deeply about the importance of each. I also provide a glimpse into how I attempt to employ these strategies in my own walk with Christ. As always, I hope everything communicated here will be of inspirational value.

Francis de Sales

As we survey the pursuit-oriented suggestions provided by Francis de Sales, keep in mind that he was writing as a spiritual director to individuals with whom he had been in close contact. This explains the ethos of interpersonal familiarity in de Sales' prescriptions. Though his work *Introduction to the Devout Life,* written in

1608, requires some transposition in order to be applied to life as it is experienced today, the suggestions he offers possess an enduring quality.

✠ We should meditate often on the life and passion of Christ.

> I especially counsel you to practice mental prayer, the prayer of the heart, and particularly that which centers on the life and passion of our Lord. By often turning your eyes on him in meditation, your whole soul will be filled with him. You will learn his ways and form your actions after the pattern of his.[7]

Perhaps it goes without saying that our souls should be filled with Christ. A basic way to achieve this is by a frequent, prayer-filled focus on what the Gospels say about the way Jesus lived his life and how he suffered for the sake of others. But does such meditation automatically result in spiritual formation? While I believe the honest answer is no, we should note that de Sales goes on to insist the following:

✠ We should begin and end each prayer intending to connect with God rather than to simply perform a necessary ritual.

> Begin all your prayers, whether mental or vocal, in the presence of God.[8] Keep to this rule without any exception and you will quickly see how helpful it will be.[9]

⊠ We should learn to move as seamlessly as possible from prayer to our everyday activities.

You must even accustom yourself to know how to pass from prayer to all the various duties your vocation and state of life rightfully and lawfully require of you, even though they may appear far different from the affections you received in prayer. I mean that the lawyer must be able to pass from prayer to pleading cases, the merchant to commerce, and the married woman to her duties as wife and her household tasks with so much ease and tranquility that their minds are not disturbed. Since both prayer and your other duties are in conformity with God's will, you must pass from one to the other with a devout and humble mind.[10]

I appreciate the way this spiritual director encouraged his mentorees to do that which is necessary to connect their formal prayer times with the other activities that make up their days, doing their best in the process to overcome any sort of sacred/secular antithesis. Toward this end, he makes three other important suggestions:

⊠ We should learn to retreat often into the solitude of our hearts, even when we are surrounded by people.

Always remember . . . to retire at various times into the solitude of your own heart even while outwardly engaged in discussion or transactions with others. This mental solitude cannot be violated by the many people who surround you since they are not standing around your heart but only around your body. Your heart remains alone in the presence of God.[11]

✠ We should recognize the value of short, extemporaneous, heartfelt prayers and employ them often.

Make spiritual aspirations to God by short, ardent movements of your heart. . . . Marvel at this beauty, implore his help, cast yourself in spirit at the foot of the cross, adore his goodness, converse often with him about your salvation, present your soul to him a thousand times during the day, fix your interior eyes upon his sweet countenance, stretch out your hand to him like a child to his father so that he may lead you on. Place him in your bosom like a fragrant bouquet, plant him in your heart like a flag, and make a thousand different motions of your heart to provide you with love of God and arouse in yourself a passionate and tender affection for this divine Spouse.[12]

✠ We should learn to keep one eye (and ear) open to the Lord, even as we engage in activities that would seem to require all our attention.

In ordinary affairs and occupations that do not require strict, earnest attention, you should look at God rather than at them. When they are of such importance as to require your whole attention to do them well, then too you should look from time to time at God, like mariners who to arrive at the port they are bound for look at the sky above them rather than down on the sea on which they sail. Thus God will work with you, in you, and for you, and after your labor consolation will follow.[13]

As a Roman Catholic who believed that, during the Mass, the bread and wine are transformed into the body and blood of Jesus, de Sales was convinced that via prayerful participation in the Eucharist the follower of Jesus comes into contact with Christ's real (corporeal) presence. This belief led him to make the following suggestion:

✠ We should observe the Lord's Supper on a consistent, frequent basis.

> Always keep yourself close to Jesus Christ crucified, both spiritually by meditation and really by Holy Communion.[14]

Though writing as a Protestant evangelical, I essentially agree that it's possible to approach our observance of the Lord's Supper as a spiritual discipline. One does not have to hold to the doctrine of transubstantiation to sense an empowering presence of the risen Christ during the Communion service. Many Protestants embrace the notion that interaction with a *spiritual* presence of Jesus should accompany our attempts to obey the biblical call to remember him (see 1 Corinthians 11:23–25). Thus, I would encourage more of my evangelical colleagues to keep "the pursuit" in mind as they endeavor to participate prayerfully and meaningfully in the ritual of Communion.

Frank Laubach

We've already taken note of the somewhat quirky manner in which Frank Laubach approaches his discussion of "the pursuit." So, it shouldn't surprise us that he sometimes refers to this spiritual exercise as a "game with minutes." I don't suspect his choice of words was reflective of a flippant attitude toward the holy habit we've been studying. Instead, because Laubach took the pursuit of Christ's empowering presence so seriously, he wanted to make the endeavor as interesting as possible to his readers.

In any case, keeping Laubach's "game" rhetoric in mind can help us better understand the challenging—and, frankly, sometimes edgy—nature of his strategic counsel. One thing is for sure: if anyone fails in his or her engagement in "the pursuit," it won't be because Laubach didn't make the ground rules for this contest clear. Of the many specific suggestions put forward in Laubach's writings on Christian spirituality, presented here are the ones I consider the most interesting and helpful.

✠ We should immerse ourselves in ministry to others rather than remaining preoccupied with our own needs.

> So if anybody were to ask me how to find God I should say at once, hunt out the deepest need you can find and forget all about your own comfort while you try to meet that need. Talk to God about it, and—he will be there. You will know it.[15]

According to this somewhat counterintuitive but very important ground rule, we experience God's presence best not by seeking it per se, but by becoming involved in ministries he cares about and we can't possibly accomplish without his assistance. Vaguely reminiscent of the connection between prayer and action conceived of by Ignatius of Loyola, this approach to spirituality holds that instead of merely asking God to go wherever we go (and, by implication, to lend his support for whatever we're doing), real success at "the pursuit" requires that we sense where God is at work in the world and make the quality decision to partner with him there!

✠ We should make it a habit to talk about God to other people.

> The week with its failures and successes has taught me one new lesson. It is this: "I must talk about God, or I cannot

keep Him in my mind. I must give Him away in order to have Him." That is the law of the spirit world. What one gives one has, what one keeps to oneself one loses.[16]

Another prerequisite for success in "the pursuit," according to Laubach, is that we not keep it a secret. We must let others know of our love for the Lord and why we're so eager to maintain an intimate, interactive communion with him. Laubach goes so far as to refer to this as a "spiritual law." In other words, one hard-and-fast rule of the "game with minutes" is that the more we own Christ before others, the greater will be our sense of his empowering presence in our lives. Good to know!

✠ **We should keep in mind that learning to practice God's presence is like forming any other habit—it requires a real effort at the beginning, but then gets easier.**

> You will find this just as easy and just as hard as forming any other habit. You have hitherto thought of God for only a few seconds or minutes a week, and He was out of your mind the rest of the time. Now you are attempting, like Brother Lawrence, to have God in mind each minute you are awake. Such a drastic change in habit requires a real effort at the beginning.[17]

Actually, this is a theme we've come across before and may again before our journey together concludes. It's apparently a fundamental truth that more than one spiritual master felt the need to emphasize. We should not allow some initial failures at the "game with minutes" to cause us to quit. Though the pursuit of Christ's empowering presence does indeed require some serious effort in the beginning, we must hang in there, trusting that it really does become easier after a while.

✠ We should learn to interpret everything beautiful in nature as God speaking to us.

If you are strolling out of doors alone, you can recall God at least once every minute with no effort, if you remember that "beauty is the voice of God." Every flower, every tree, river and lake, mountain and sunset, is God speaking, "This is my Father's world, and to my listening ears all nature sings. . . ." So as you look at each lovely thing, you may keep asking: "Dear Father, what are you telling me through this, and this, and this?"[18]

A careful reading of Laubach will indicate how big he was on sensing God's presence in the world around him. In the quote presented above, he states, "beauty is the voice of God." This is one of the most profound concepts I've come across in my reading of the spiritual masters, and it has made a huge difference in my own spirituality. I'll say more about this in the next chapter where I provide some detail about my own engagement in "the pursuit."

In the meantime, here's a final strategic suggestion provided by Laubach.

✠ We should take seriously the costs involved in a serious engagement in "the pursuit."

In this final quote, Laubach provides a brief discussion of the price that must be paid in order to be successful at the "game with minutes." Here's his short list:

The first price is pressure of our wills, gentle but constant. What game is ever won without concentration?

The second price is perseverance. A low score at the onset is not the least reason for discouragement; everybody gets a low score for a long while. Each week grows better and requires less strain.

The third price is perfect surrender. We lose Christ the moment our wills rebel. If we try to keep even a remote corner of life for self or evil, and refuse to let God rule us wholly, that small worm will spoil the entire fruit. We must be utterly sincere.

The fourth price is [the requirement that we must] tell others. When anybody complains that he is losing the game, we flash this question back at him: "Are you telling your friends about it?" For you cannot keep Christ unless you give Him away.

The fifth price is to be in a group. We need the stimulus of a few intimate friends who exchange their experiences with us.[19]

Some of these costs were also revealed in previous quotes; I want to draw your attention to two that weren't.

For one, it's important for us to wrestle with the reality that any attempt on our part to compartmentalize—to declare any area of our life off-limits to Christ—constitutes an act of self-sabotage when it comes to "the pursuit." Jesus loves us deeply, but he isn't naive. He knows when we are holding back, not truly wanting to be empowered toward Christlikeness in attitudes and actions we continue to cherish, though we know they are unholy. Frankly, I believe, along with Laubach, that a case can be made for the notion of divine discipline, even under the terms of the new covenant. Simply put, Jesus really does love us too much to allow us to hurt ourselves by trying to restrict his lordship (and sanctifying work) to just certain areas of our existence. Thus, should we find ourselves failing miserably at the "game with minutes," and doing so consistently over a long season of time, we should probably spend some time coming clean before the one we claim to want to love and serve with all our heart, mind, soul, and strength.[20]

For another, I deeply appreciate Laubach's emphasis upon the importance of community. He speaks of the need for "the stimulus of a few intimate friends who exchange their experiences with us." I would go so far as to say there's a sense in which not only is the "game with minutes" a team sport, the Christian life as a whole is one as well. To succeed at both, we really do need the ongoing support and accountability provided by a few intimate friends (see Galatians 6:1–2; Colossians 3:16; Hebrews 10:24–25; James 5:16).[21]

Jan Johnson

There isn't space in this chapter to include all the helpful pursuit-oriented suggestions provided by Jan Johnson in her book *Enjoying the Presence of God*. My sincere recommendation is that anyone who is serious about cultivating an ongoing, transformational experience of God's presence should immediately acquire this volume and begin putting it to use. That said, of the many practical suggestions Johnson includes in her work, the ones presented below have had the most impact upon my own spiritual journey.

The first of Johnson's suggestions has to do with how we approach "the pursuit" overall.

✖ We should recognize our need to ease our way into what amounts to a whole new lifestyle.

This experiment in keeping constant company with God cannot be rushed because God is doing the work in us and we cannot hurry God. We let go of the desire to perform and ease into this practice, knowing that intimacy is never instant. We are embarking on a lifelong journey of welcoming the invasion of our soul by the Holy Spirit so that moments with God are sprinkled throughout the day like manna in the desert.[22]

Essentially, this is another way of making the point that "the pursuit" is a habit like any other: it takes time and patience to develop. This quote also reminds us that the process of spiritual formation is not something we can control. Christ-followers who struggle as I do with the "hurry sickness" need to keep both of these important caveats in mind. Nothing improves my ability to slow down and "live in the moment" like a moment-by-moment pursuit of Christ's empowering presence. But to do this we must adopt a slogan familiar to those involved in a 12-step recovery program: *Easy does it!*

Speaking of living in the moment, for many, the great enemy to life in the Spirit is not hurry, but the many people with whom we are forced to share space. Like the ancient hermits who fled to the Egyptian desert, we tell ourselves that if it weren't for the distractions caused by society as a whole and certain people in particular, we could become much more spiritual in the way we conduct our affairs. Over against this notion, the next two suggestions concern ways we can actually allow life with others to improve our ability to sense Christ's presence on a moment-by-moment basis.

✠ We should develop the habit of turning our hearts toward God each time we converse with others.

As God becomes our life companion, it seems normal to invite Him to participate in our conversations with others. Frank Laubach described these experiences as "continuous silent conversations of heart to heart with God while looking into other eyes and listening to other voices." You might think this sounds like a confusing dual conversation, but it isn't. . . .

As people's motives and feelings unfold, we may see that God is working within them in ways that surprise us. . . . We

> ask God, *How can I be present for them? Is there something they need that I have to offer? How can I cooperate with You, God, in helping them pursue Your purposes for their life?*[23]

We should develop the habit of turning our hearts toward God each time we even think of others.

In the process of relating the story of an interaction with a friend, Johnson writes:

> Lynne's words, "Every time I think of him, I forgive him a little more," forged for me another small path for abiding in God's presence—offering a brief prayer every time I thought of someone. Instead of forming opinions of people—"How disgusting he is!" or "How clever she is!"—I could pray for that person. Perhaps the apostle Paul had a similar practice of praying for people when he thought of them, evidenced by his words, "I thank my God every time I remember you" (Philippians 1:3).[24]

Now I would be kidding not only my readers but myself as well if I were to suggest that I've mastered the two holy habits just alluded to. Progress, yes; perfection, no. Then again, at least I'm trying!

Ultimately, these quotes underscore the fact that one doesn't have to be a hermit to enjoy a pervasive sense of Christ's presence. Indeed, our thoughts of, and conversations with, others can actually become the means by which we experience an increased number of intimate interactions with the risen Lord each day.

With the goal of living in the moment still in view, a final suggestion offered by Johnson calls for us to engage in a particular kind of prayer.

✠ We should learn to make use of "breath prayers."

> Our back-and-forth communication with God might take the time-proven "breath prayer" format, repeating a familiar prayer of nine or ten syllables or less that has great meaning.[25]

The idea here is that we can develop the habit of calling upon Christ many times throughout each day. Each time we do, we invite the Lord to enter whatever situation has us sensing our need for divine assistance.

Francis de Sales encouraged his mentorees to use the phrase "Live, Jesus!" as a breath prayer.[26] I assume he had Galatians 2:20 in mind.

A breath prayer I often use is the classic "Jesus Prayer," which goes like this: *Lord Jesus Christ, Son of God, have mercy upon me a sinner.* For a couple of reasons this particular prayer resonates with me at a very deep level. First of all, I love the way it affirms the essential deity of the risen and ascended Christ and affords me the opportunity to affirm anew his lordship over my life. Second, even though this prayer calls for me to confess that I'm a sinner, I appreciate that it also reminds me time and again that the Jesus I serve is committed to show me mercy, he has personally paid the price necessary to effect my salvation, and he presently deigns to function for me as a great high priest and advocate before the Father.

Given the post-conservative, post-Christian era in which we live, I consider these to be some pretty important Christological commitments. Can we be reminded too often of the need to live our lives based on them? Personally, I don't think so. Not if we want to cultivate a spirituality that is more than a form of godliness (see 2 Timothy 3:5), that can produce within us the ironically powerful humility before God and others that Jesus possessed, and that a "Colossians 3 kind of life" requires.

John Ortberg

In his book *God Is Closer Than You Think,* John Ortberg writes, "Now let's get very concrete. If we want to spend a regular ordinary day of our life *with Jesus,* what would we actually do? How do we go about trying to receive each moment as a sacrament, a God-charged sliver of grace?"[27] Ortberg goes on to stipulate, "Spending the day with God does not usually involve doing different things from what we already do. Mostly it involves learning to do what we already do in a new way—*with God.*"[28] Then he walks us through the main events of a typical day, indicating how we might practice God's presence during each.

In addition to his helpful encouragements to offer to God our "washing up" routine as a symbolic, sacramental act,[29] to revive the once-popular ritual of interacting with God during mealtimes,[30] and to be creative in the way we share with Jesus all the "odds and ends" moments of each day (paying bills, running errands, and so forth),[31] Ortberg offers several other suggestions that merit special attention.

✠ We should begin each day doing our best to connect with God.

Try to arrange—as early as you can after you wake up—to have just a few minutes alone with God. Do three things:

1. Acknowledge your dependence on God. *I won't live through this day banking on my own strength and power.*

2. Tell God about your concerns for the day, and ask him to identify and remove any fear in you. I often do this with my calendar for the day open before me.

3. Renew your invitation for God to spend the day with you.[32]

This appears to be sound advice, doesn't it? If our goal is to experience an ongoing sense of Christ's presence throughout the day, then it has to begin sometime. Why not as early in the day as possible?

That said, how many minutes do you think such a centering routine would require? I suggest it doesn't have to take a long time. I realize how busy many of us are and how we may feel the need to "hit the ground running." But please don't allow a sense of early-morning hurry keep you from spending just a few moments becoming centered in Christ as soon as possible each day of your life.

✠ We should be careful to learn how to do our work together with Jesus.

As Jesus' friends, we start our workday by inviting him to be present with us. I generally start work by sitting at my desk, reviewing my meetings and tasks for the day, and—instead of just worrying about them—asking God if we can partner together in them. . . .

Every few hours I try to remember to take a break. That may be something as simple as sitting up straight and taking a few deep breaths; as I breathe, I remember that I am being filled with God's Spirit. I may look out the window at something growing outside, or listen to music that speaks to my soul. . . .

At the end of my workday I used to become discouraged at what I didn't accomplish. Now I try to do what God did during the week of creation: to look at what has been accomplished that day and celebrate what is good. I thank God that he has partnered with me through the day. I take a moment to ask him to partner with me tomorrow.[33]

It's not that we haven't already established the fact that it's possible to commune with Christ even as we engage in our occupational activities; several of the ancient spiritual masters we've surveyed have made this point. Still, I find it interesting to read how a very busy contemporary Christian professional—one who admits to struggling with a tendency toward hurry—routinely attempts to pull this off.

Then again, perhaps you're wondering whether you can trust Ortberg's description of this aspect of his day. Maybe his spiritual counsel sounds just a bit too "spiritual" to be true. Though I'm sure some aspects of our personalities and work styles differ, I "hear" and "feel" what Ortberg is saying in the passages cited above. Furthermore, I can assure you that it is possible to develop a raised consciousness regarding this issue. Though neither Ortberg nor I claim to have this mastered, we *know* that with the help of the Holy Spirit it is possible to possess a heightened awareness of, and desire for, a sense of Christ's empowering presence even while being very busy at work. You don't have to be Brother Lawrence working in a monastery kitchen to experience God on the job!

✠ We should do our best to see interruptions and occasions when we're forced to wait as providential (rather than accidental or diabolical) and respond to them appropriately.

It is possible that when the phone rings or there's a knock on the door or somebody wants a favor or I see a person with a flat tire on the side of the road, it is a divine appointment. God has come close.

Standing in line—which always feels like an interruption to my schedule—no longer has to be an exercise in frustration for me. It can become (and sometimes does—not always, but sometimes) a moment when I look at my fellow standers and talk to God about them and say silent prayers of blessing for them. For some of them, that may be the only prayer they receive all day.[34]

Again, at first this may sound too good to be true. It's not. Remember, Ortberg admits that he's not always on his game; sometimes he fails to practice the disciplines he advocates. But just because something is hard doesn't mean it's impossible. We really can become more patient, spiritually centered people, attentive to divine breathings precisely because we're sensitive to the needs of those around us. This is a big part of living in the moment. It really is possible. The pursuit of Christ's empowering presence is the key.

Dallas Willard

Given the obvious influence Dallas Willard has had upon my understanding of Christian spirituality, you had to know that some of his practical counsel would be included in this chapter. The quotes presented below are very rich. I hope you'll read and reread them over and again until the essence of them is absorbed into your heart as well as your mind.

The first prescription proffered by Willard is yet another version of the exhortation to carefully consider how we begin our days.

We should begin each day committing it to the Lord's care; then go into it counting on his very real assistance.

> Jesus' resurrected presence with us, along with his teaching, assures us of God's care for all who let him be God and let him care for them. "Do not be afraid, little flock, for your Father has chosen gladly to give you the kingdom" (Luke 12:32). It is love of God, admiration and confidence in his greatness and goodness, and regular experience of his care that frees us from the burden of "looking out for ourselves."
>
> What remarkable changes this introduces into our day-to-day life! Personally, at the beginning of my day—often

before arising—I commit my day to the Lord's care. Usually I do this while meditatively praying through the Lord's Prayer, and possibly the twenty-third Psalm as well. Then I meet everything that happens as sent or at least permitted by God. I meet it resting in the hand of his care. This helps me to "do all things without grumbling or disputing" (Philippians 2:14), because I have already "placed God in charge" and am trusting him to manage them for my good. I no longer have to manage the weather, airplanes, and other people.[35]

When my wife, Patti, was reading over the manuscript for this book, she was especially struck by the quote just cited. Frankly, her reaction is precisely the type I'm hoping for from all who read this work. Isn't it inspiring to think that someday we might come to the place where our spirituality enables us to trust that, having given our day over to God, we can proceed into it with a heart filled with faith rather than fear? You know you want this! Right?

Going further, another key to engaging successfully in "the pursuit," says Willard, is to fill our minds with the truth of Scripture. Thus, he suggests the following:

✠ We should make it a point to memorize and meditate often on key portions of Scripture.

There are certain tried-and-true disciplines we can use to aid in the transformation of our thought life toward the mind of Christ. . . .

The most obvious thing we can do is to draw certain key portions of Scripture into our minds and make them a part of the permanent fixtures of our thought. This is the primary discipline for the thought life. We need to know them like the back of our hand, and a good way to do that is to memorize them and then constantly turn them over in our minds as we go through the events and circumstances of our life (Joshua 1:8; Psalm 1).[36]

Bible memory work isn't something only kids in Sunday school and Vacation Bible School should do. We're never too old to spend quality time committing some especially critical biblical passages into our memory, so they can daily influence our actions and attitudes.

During the two-week "Spirituality and Ministry" seminar I attended eight years ago, Willard exhorted all his doctoral students to memorize Colossians 3:1–17. A careful reading of *Renovation of the Heart* might suggest other passages upon which we might focus: Romans 12:1–21; 1 Corinthians 13:1–13; 2 Corinthians 3:12–7:1; Galatians 5:22–6:10; Ephesians 4:20–6:20; Philippians 2:3–16; 4:4–9; 1 Peter 2:1–3:16; 2 Peter 1:2–10; and 1 John 4:7–21.[37]

We shouldn't allow the length of some of these Bible portions to intimidate us. Though it may be more difficult to accomplish the older we get, it is not impossible to memorize huge chunks of God's Word, meditating deeply upon the truths they contain during the process and ever after. I'll say more about this particular discipline in the next chapter.

Finally, congratulations! A very important pursuit-oriented suggestion put forward by Willard is actually something you've been doing ever since you picked up this book! As it relates to the goal of cultivating a healthy Christian spirituality, Willard is emphatic that . . .

We should become familiar with the methods used by both contemporary and historical models.

> You need to *seek out* others in your community who are pursuing the renovation of the heart. . . . We must pray that God will lead us to others who can walk with us with Christ—whoever and wherever they may be. And then in patience stay with them.

> This will naturally lead to . . . the identification of
> older practitioners of The Way [i.e., the masters]. We need
> to understand those who have learned how to live with a
> transformed mind and study carefully what they did—not
> necessarily in order to do exactly what they did, for they are
> not lawgivers, nor are they always right, much less perfect.
> But we cannot easily or wisely dispense with what they have
> learned and what can be learned from them. . . .
>
> How did they come to be able to live with "the Lord
> always before them"? We learn from them how to do that by
> making them our close companions on the way.[38]

As I've said many times in these pages, one of my goals has been
to help us "master the masters." Is there a sense in which you've come
to think of folks such as Brother Lawrence, Francis de Sales, Jeremy
Taylor, Frank Laubach, and John Ortberg as "close companions on
the way"? I certainly hope so.

As Willard suggests, I too hope you will identify some spiritually hungry pilgrims much closer to home so that you won't have to
make this journey alone. Toward this end, I encourage you to keep
sharing this book with family members, church members, and work
associates until you've formed a small cadre of Christ-followers who
share your passion for "the pursuit" and who will walk with you as
you endeavor to walk with Christ (see Ecclesiastes 4:9–12).

Then again, our partnership in this journey hasn't completely
run its course. There's one more thing I can do to function for you as
a "close companion on the way." In the next chapter, the last of this
book, I invite you to get up close and personal as I share some personal details regarding my devotional routine and how, throughout
a typical day, I attempt to maintain a sense of Christ's empowering
presence. Will my personal sharing prove helpful to your own engagement in "the pursuit"? There's only one way to find out.

9

LIFTING THE VEIL:
MY OWN APPROACH TO
"THE PURSUIT"

I've been arguing in this book that "the pursuit" is at the heart of Christian spirituality and should therefore be integral to all the other spiritual disciplines in which we engage. John Ortberg's helpful description of what the various spiritual disciplines accomplish in our lives offers tacit support for this thesis:

> Spiritual disciplines are not self-improvement techniques. They are not activities I do for spiritual extra-credit. They are what John Wesley called "means of grace." In 12-step terms, they always involve letting go. The Bible's word for that is surrender.
>
> They help me submit my will to the divine will. They are like a cord that plugs an otherwise inert appliance into a source of power. They connect me to a reality deeper and more powerful than myself. Ultimately, they connect me to Jesus. They help me access the life that flows only from him.[1]

As we near the end of our journey, I want to "lift the veil" to provide a glimpse into my own approach to "the pursuit" and how it plays out during a typical day in my life. What follows, however, is not a thorough treatment of how I engage in every spiritual discipline. As important as all the spiritual disciplines are to my experience of Christ's empowering presence—fasting, celebration, corporate worship, simplicity, sacrifice, service, secrecy, and others—the truth is that my engagement in them is less frequent. There are, nevertheless, some spiritual disciplines—some centering activities—that I do employ most every day (while doing my best not to do so in a rigid, inflexible, legalistic manner). These are the spiritual exercises I want to describe briefly and advocate for in the pages that follow. Though the authors we surveyed in the previous chapter referred to some of these exercises, I'll indicate here my own approach to them and the unique effects they tend to produce in my life.

Before we get started, however, I admit to being more than a little reticent to speak of these matters for two reasons. First, I certainly don't want to be misunderstood as suggesting that the way I endeavor to maintain a sense of Christ's empowering presence is the way everyone should. I'm in complete agreement with John Ortberg when he says,

> Many approaches to spiritual growth assume the same methods will produce the same growth in different people—but they don't. Because you have been created by God as a unique person, his plan to grow you will not look the same as his plan to grow anyone else. . . .
>
> God never grows two people the exact same way. God is a hand-crafter, not a mass-producer.
>
> The problem many people face when it comes to spiritual growth is that they listen to someone they think of as an expert—maybe an author or radio personality—talk about what he does and they think that's what they're supposed to

do. When it doesn't work for them (because they are a different person!) they feel guilty and inadequate, and often give up.

> God has a plan for the me he wants me to be. It will not look exactly like his plan for anyone else, which means it will take freedom and exploration for you to learn how God wants to grow you. Spiritual growth is hand-crafted, not mass-produced. God does not do "one-size-fits-all."[2]

So please don't make the mistake of hearing me say this is the way you too must endeavor to become and remain centered in Christ throughout your days. This is simply my way. If something I do sounds interesting and potentially helpful, experiment with it yourself. If not, don't worry about it. Keep exploring in order to discover your own unique method of engaging in "the pursuit."

A second reason for my reticence to share my story is based upon the recognition that, according to Jesus' Sermon on the Mount, we should not parade our spirituality before others (Matthew 6:1–18). While I'll do my best not to expound upon my daily devotional practices in any sort of boastful manner, there's a sense in which I'm going public with some things that are normally supposed to be done in secret. My confidence in doing this is that God knows my heart. I'm certain he's aware that, to the best of my knowledge, my motive in pulling back the curtain to share some of the details regarding my own spirituality is genuinely altruistic rather than self-serving. If the truth is otherwise, I pray that both God and my readers will forgive me.

So, with all these caveats firmly in place, what follows is a fairly brief but honest reflection on my own imperfect attempts to maintain an intimate, interactive walk with Christ.

Crucial Centering Activities in the Morning

Following the lead of Dallas Willard, I've developed the habit of beginning most days prayerfully reciting the Lord's Prayer and

Psalm 23. Doing so before I get completely out of bed strikes me as simply the right thing to do. This simple devotional practice has me offering the firstfruits of my time and attention to the creator and sustainer of the universe (Romans 12:1). It also enables me to turn over each day, before it even gets started, to a divine being whom the Bible encourages me to conceive of as a loving father and caring shepherd. Thus, I can rise from the side of my bed and enter into this new mini-season of my existence confident that I live in a "good-God-governed universe" and that I don't have to worry about how every event is going to play out. Ultimately, I'm not in charge of this day; God is. And over the years he's proven himself to be really good at causing all things to work together for good (see Romans 8:28).

Though I'm still a long, long way from becoming as worry-free as Jesus would have me (see Matthew 6:25–34), over time I'm making progress toward that goal. Honestly, it's hard for me to imagine what kind of person I would be sans the comforting, guiding, hope-producing relationship I have with the risen Christ. At the same time, I've come to realize how vital it is for me to become centered in Christ each morning if I am to take full advantage of this empowering relationship. Thanks to the encouragement of Dallas Willard, I've found that the simple routine described above is a great way to do so.

A Formal Time of Study

After coming downstairs and acquiring my first cup of coffee, I routinely attempt to strengthen my connection with Christ by spending thirty to forty minutes reading and studying God's Word.[3] For over eight years now my habit has been to read five chapters from the Book of Psalms each morning, thus reading through the entire collection every month. There's something about a meditative, repetitive reading of these Spirit-inspired prayers of petition, praise, and lament that helps me enter most days with "the pursuit" on my mind. Likewise, reading one chapter from the Book of Proverbs each morning not only enables me to process this entire catalog of wisdom sayings each month, but it also prepares me to face the day with some sage advice still ringing in my spiritual ears. Finally, each morning I also read at least one chapter, often more, from both Testaments.

As I engage in this Bible reading (always with pencil in hand, marking passages, writing notes in the margins), my goal is to discern how the Holy Spirit (and the human author) would have hoped that the original readers of these texts would have understood and responded to them. At the same time, I'm continually on the lookout for some sense that it might be God's desire to "speak" to me in a special, existential, immediate manner through this or that portion of his Word.

Not feeling the need to read through the Bible on any sort of schedule (though I usually end up doing so every year and a half to two years), I sometimes feel led to engage in a repetitive reading of the same section of Scripture for several days. This practice allows me to meditate deeply upon a passage I feel the Holy Spirit has prompted me to focus upon. Usually it doesn't take long for events to transpire that enable me to recognize why I needed to spend some extended time studying this or that particular passage. The Spirit was preparing me for what was ahead in my spiritual and ministry journey!

Similarly, I've also profited greatly from the practice of Scripture memorization, which is an even more intense form of meditative study. Occasionally I feel especially impressed to study a portion of Scripture by committing it to memory. To be honest, my ability to recite some of the longer passages I've memorized over the past thirty-five years doesn't last forever. For example, on a moment's notice I could not adequately recite for anyone the entirety of the Sermon on the Mount, Romans 8, Colossians 3, or the Epistle to the Ephesians. Still, I'm convinced that the time and energy I once spent committing these passages to memory has greatly aided my understanding of them. In my experience, once I've grappled with the "spirit" of a biblical text, through meditative memorization, the interpretive insights generated by this method of study become part of me forever!

The bottom line is that all these forms of devotional Bible reading have been very effective at slowing me down and helping me become centered in God as I begin my day. I can't state this emphatically enough: *there's a huge difference between truly connecting with Christ during my morning quiet times and simply getting through them out of some sense of pietistic obligation!*

After this prayerful, meditative study of Scripture is concluded, my custom is to round out the first hour of my day with a second cup of coffee and a few minutes spent dipping into whatever book on spirituality, theology, or ministry I happen to be working through at the time. It's amazing how many great books we can prayerfully interact with in this manner over the course of a year!

A Formal (Sort of) Engagement in Prayer and Worship

What follows this daily time of study (see 2 Timothy 2:15) is a centering activity that, while hard to label, has proved to be a very important component of my spiritual formation. Because it's still early in the day (my habit is to begin devotional exercises around five o'clock each morning) and my work schedule allows it, and because I live in Southern California where the weather is usually accommodating, I'm able most mornings to continue praying as I take my dog, Jack (a very bright Border collie), for a two-mile walk. These long walks provide me with an opportunity to experience a short but significant season of solitude that often produces some really profound effects.

First, during these jaunts I formally invite Christ to be part of every item on that day's agenda—classes, meetings, counseling appointments, writing sessions, and so forth. I lift before the Lord any activity or responsibility that calls for even a modicum of creativity or prophetic capacity and ask him to provide it. While I'll stop short of referring to them as "inspired," the fact is that some of the most insightful and effective strategies I've ever come up with have derived from these times of prayerful communion.

Second, this long hike is also an occasion to converse with the Lord about specific worrisome concerns bouncing around in my brain. Though I'd like to say that this prayer practice never fails to produce within me an overriding sense of peace, the truth is that some days I return to the house as burdened as I was when I left. *Most of the time,* however, my anxiety is greatly assuaged as I pour out my heart to my invisible walking partner. I'm convinced that my anxiety eases because I lift these issues before the Lord, praying in the Spirit according to Romans 8:26–27 (see also 1 Corinthians 14:15; Ephesians 6:18; Jude 20) and asking Jesus to impart to me the same wisdom, courage, and compassion that seemed to earmark his earthly existence. Many mornings I also feel led to express to the Lord my longing to know afresh—to *really know,* deep inside, at the core of my being—just how much I am loved by him (see Ephesians 3:16–19), so that I might "live" in his love and share it with others. I've found it nearly impossible to utter this prayer *sincerely* without immediately experiencing a wonderful, peace-producing sense of Christ's empowering presence.

Speaking of loving others, these daily walks are, thirdly, times to pray for family members, friends, students, and colleagues, mentally lifting them before the Lord. Often I imagine the life-giving light of God's face shining upon each of these folks, one after the other (see Psalm 4:6; 67:1; 80:3, 7, 19). If I know of a specific need in their lives, I will intercede, asking God to address that particular issue with kingdom power in Jesus' name. If I'm not aware of a specific need, I petition God on their behalf, once again engaging in that spiritual discipline the New Testament refers to as "praying in the Spirit."

Fourth, when I'm at my best, I whisper intercessory prayers for the people whose paths I cross during the course of each day's trek. Usually I pray that if these folks are not believers, the Holy Spirit will help them recognize the glory of God in the face of Christ Jesus (2 Corinthians 4:3–6); if they are believers, I ask the Lord to bless them and make them missionally effective in the cause of Christ.

I'm especially prompted to engage in this kind of anonymous intercession when my first impulse is to think of someone I encounter in an impure or unkind manner. Yes, it happens! On any given day, I might be tempted to ogle an attractive female jogger or to form a negative opinion of the guy who thinks he's the only person in the world who doesn't need to keep his dog on a leash! I'm doing my best to become intentional about *praying for people* rather than simply *thinking about them*. The sixth chapter of Paul's Epistle to the Romans seems to teach that the key to defeating old, unrighteous habits is to replace them with new, righteous ones. How great it would be if our first impulse when meeting a new person was to respond to him or her the way Jesus would! I'm still working on that, encouraged by the thought that even baby steps can still represent progress in the right direction.

Finally, prayer is not the only spiritual discipline enabled by these daily walks. Along with Frank Laubach, I've come to believe that the sublime beauty we find in nature is a subtle but powerful way in which God speaks to us and prompts us to acknowledge him.[4] Simply put, the world doesn't have to be as beautiful as it is. Furthermore, I believe that the best explanation for the aesthetic sensibilities present in our hearts is that a creative God placed them there. Whenever we see or hear something extraordinarily beautiful or complex (or both) in the world around us, it's possible to be reminded of the Creator's power and providential care for those who share his image. Thus these long walks often lead me into profound experiences of not only prayer, but of worship as well. (I'll say more below about the importance of worship to "the pursuit.")

I fully recognize that I probably need to build into my busy schedule some extended seasons of solitude during which I can disengage from society and simply *be* in the presence of God. The fact is that my present pursuit of Christ's empowering presence *is* tremendously enriched each day by the half-hour of solitude I experience during these long walks. I heartily recommend this practice to anyone whose circumstances will allow it.[5]

Centering Activities at Work

We've seen that a great number of Christian spiritual masters have made a point to encourage the practice of carrying a sense of Christ's presence "from the cell or chapel to the kitchen"—that is, from the devotional space to the place of work. Here's how I routinely attempt to follow this important spiritual counsel.

The Morning Commute

During my morning commute to the university (about half an hour on average), I continue to pray over my day and for various acquaintances as they come to mind. And driving on the freeways of Southern California affords me plenty of other opportunities to intercede anonymously for folks, especially for those I'm tempted to curse rather than bless because of their discourteous or dangerous driving, or for those I hear about on the radio who've been injured in auto accidents. When the traffic slows to a stop and I feel myself beginning to stress, I try to remember to take some deep breaths and focus on the fact that Jesus is there in the car with me. What a great opportunity to commune with him!

The Workday Proper

Once I've arrived at the university and parked my car, I often have the presence of mind to invite Jesus to walk with me toward my office and into my workday. This represents yet another opportunity to imagine the remainder of the day and what it would be like to experience Christ's empowering presence during every part of it.

Throughout the day, then, I often think to pause just long enough to reckon with Christ's abiding presence and to solicit his support and guidance regarding the task at hand. It's in this way that I've discovered how much more peaceful life is, and how much more efficient I am, when I commune with Christ all day long, instead of confining my experience of him to a morning and/or evening quiet time.

To be more specific, interactions with others, scheduled and unscheduled, are a big part of my everyday life. When conversations center upon spiritual themes, they obviously reinforce my focus on Christ and his kingdom. But even when a conversation is not "spiritual," I sometimes remember to turn my heart toward Christ and experience his empowering presence as a result.

When I'm involved in scheduled counseling or mentoring conversations, this ability to pray inwardly, reckoning with Christ's presence and expressing my need for his wisdom, has proved invaluable time and again. The same can be said for impromptu chats or counseling sessions. Like John Ortberg and Jan Johnson, I'm learning to interpret these "interruptions" as "divine appointments"—unexpected opportunities to make a difference for good in someone's life. My habit during these unscheduled interactions is to inwardly ask the Lord questions such as "OK, God, what are you up to in this person's life?" "How can I cooperate with what you're doing in him or her?" "Are you up to something in *my* life through this unplanned conversation? How can I cooperate with that?" Though this response to interruptions doesn't exactly come easily to someone who suffers from the "hurry sickness," I can attest that it does become easier and more consistent with practice.

Turning inward to converse with Christ is something I also do in the classroom. Earlier today, as one of my students opened a class session in prayer, I was inwardly, fervently inviting the risen Christ to be present in the class and to help me communicate in a clear, coherent, compelling manner. He did. He does.

Of course, it's one thing to experience Christ's empowering presence when I'm engaged in activities that are a joy to perform—such as preaching, teaching, counseling, writing, walking, spending time with family, and so forth. It's another thing to sense God's help when I'm forced to perform some mundane or unpleasant task, or simply to stand in line and wait. I'm discovering, however, that with a little practice we really can develop the habit of offering the most onerous chores (even waiting in line or traffic) to the Lord as a discipline, meditating in the process upon Christ's spiritual presence.

Don't get me wrong. I'm not as consistent at this as I want to be. But I've experienced this dynamic enough to recognize how just a small shift in perspective, from the earthly to the heavenly (see Colossians 3:1–4), can enable us to do all kinds of things in Christ's name (see Colossians 3:17)!

Finally, I want to say a bit more, as promised, about the vital importance of maintaining throughout the day an attitude of real gratitude to God for his many blessings. We've already seen that a good number of the classic works on Christian spirituality emphasize the important relationship between the practice of the presence of God and an ongoing engagement in worship, praise, and thanksgiving. I want to underscore that the connection between giving thanks to God and experiencing his presence is not only *correlative,* but *causative* as well. We all know how easy it is to worship and give thanks during those wonderful moments when Christ's presence is palpably evident to us (see Ephesians 5:18–20). That's what I mean when I say the presence of God and the act of giving thanks just seem to go together, to *correlate*.

But what about those times when the divine presence is not so patently obvious to us—those seasons of spiritual dryness referred to by spiritual life authors such as Thomas à Kempis and Richard Foster? While I heartily endorse what à Kempis, Foster, and others have said about the value of simply and patiently waiting these seasons out, when a sense of Christ's nearness is noticeably absent in my life, the *spiritual discipline* of giving thanks to God—in an intentional, proactive, yet sincere manner—often brings about a fresh season of his existential proximity. In other words, I suggest that the act of giving thanks in the face of our ambiguous, perhaps even adverse, circumstances can actually *cause* or facilitate a renewed sense of Christ's empowering presence.

In Psalm 50:23 we read, "He who sacrifices thank offerings honors me, and he prepares the way so that I may show him the salvation of God." I'm more than intrigued with the idea that giving thanks in a deliberate, proactive manner can somehow precipitate God's providential involvement in my life—I'm convinced of it! While I don't mean for this to be understood as a foolproof formula, because of passages such as Psalm 50:23 and because I've experienced both the correlative and causative connections between giving thanks and experiencing God's presence, *one of the grand goals of my life is to become a truly praiseful person—a man whose lifestyle is earmarked by the habit of seeing God in everything that happens, and giving him thanks, sometimes by raw faith, as a result* (see also Ephesians 5:19–20; Philippians 4:4–7; 1 Thessalonians 5:16–18). Deep inside, don't you want to become a perpetually praiseful person too?

Centering Activities in the Evening

I've discovered that it's important not to allow my commitment to engage in "the pursuit" to taper off near the end of the day. Just because I'm weary from having expended a lot of physical and mental energy at work doesn't mean that Jesus is too tired to continue mentoring me or that I no longer need his empowering presence in my life.

The Commute Home

My forty-five- to sixty-minute commute home each evening provides me with an opportunity to reflect on the quality of the day's work and, in the process, to express my great need for Christ's involvement in everything I'm responsible to accomplish, much of which is way over my head. Indeed, sometimes I'm tempted to think that an important key to a vibrant experience of "the pursuit" is to intentionally place ourselves in situations where we desperately need to manifest the same kind of wisdom, courage, and compassion we see in the life of Jesus or else we will fall flat on our faces! There's nothing like a sense of existential desperation (floundering in the deep end of the pool) to turn us into prayerful, pursuit-oriented people!

Furthermore, this time of communion with Christ during my evening commute serves to mitigate my tendency to bring work-related concerns home with me. To the degree I can "process" with Christ these problems on the way home, the less able they are to negatively impact my interaction with others the remainder of the day. Again, I don't always succeed at this; I could do better. I could also do worse! I have to keep telling myself that the key concept is . . . baby steps!

The Best Time of the Day

Once home, the evening meal I share with Patti—my best friend and wife for over thirty-five years—is always prefaced with a season of prayer during which one or both of us will invariably offer thanks to God for his gracious provision and beseech his blessing on behalf of those we know and love. This is more than a perfunctory ritual. It's a meaningful routine, one that has "the pursuit" at its center.

After a significant season of talking together during and after dinner, the rest of a typical weekday evening is usually devoted to either writing or enjoying a movie or some television (our nest is empty these days). While I can't say that we purposefully imagine Jesus sitting on the couch viewing the television along with us, a latent but genuine awareness of his loving presence is there just the same.

Patti and I really do try to allow a sense of Christ's resurrection reality to influence our speech and actions toward each other and others. When we mess up, and we still do from time to time, we eventually apologize to one another as well as to the Lord. We've worked hard over the years to cultivate what we refer to as a transformational marriage—a relationship that enables both partners to become better, more Christlike people.[6] For this to happen, a husband and wife have to function as accountability partners for each other, as well as best friends and lovers. We've found that a mutual commitment to the pursuit of Christ's empowering presence is key to all the above.

The Day's Denouement

Finally, a little later on, after having done my best all day long to maintain a sense of intimate interaction with the risen Christ, just before I drift off to sleep, my custom is to conclude the day by once again expressing my gratitude to God for his many blessings and by thanking him in advance for the privilege of waking to a fresh sense of his life-giving presence a few hours later (see Psalm 17:15; 139:18). What a sweet, satisfying time this is.

And then, sure enough, the next morning the joyful, exciting process of engaging in "the pursuit" begins all over again!

Now Is the Time to Get in the Game

In these ways, I'm doing my best to practice what I've preached the last eight years and what I'm writing about now. As I've indicated before, I'm still a million miles from where I want to be, but a fair distance down the road from where I once was. I haven't spoken here of how occasionally engaging in other spiritual disciplines—such as fasting, celebration, corporate worship, confession, submission, sacrifice, service, secrecy—is also part of my spiritual "rule." But I hope that something in the preceding pages will inspire you to make the pursuit of Christ's empowering presence the cornerstone of your own approach to being formed into the image of Christ. Because of the experiences described in this book—even the "dark night of the soul" experiences—I firmly believe that this particular spiritual exercise is the key to a "Colossians 3 kind of life" and is at the heart of Christian spirituality.

But you've known for some time now what I believe and why. Because our journey together is nearly complete, the time is drawing near for you to decide what *you* believe and how *you* will put that belief into practice. Perhaps you've already done this, already begun your own participation in "the pursuit." Good for you!

On the other hand, it could be that you're still evaluating my argument, or simply delaying—for whatever reason—your own engagement in this most basic of spiritual exercises. Just in case, I want to finish this final chapter by drawing your attention once again to Frank Laubach's quirky concept of the "game with minutes." As you recall, the goal of this "game" is to increase the amount of time each day that you are conscious of Christ's real presence in your life. What's my point? Just this: the clock *is* ticking. I'm not trying to *hurry* you, but isn't it time for you to get off the sidelines and into the "game"? Please keep this important question in mind as you carefully ponder the formal conclusion of this work, which is presented in the next few pages.

CONCLUSION

Leslie Weatherhead, writing a generation ago in his book *The Transforming Friendship,* indicates what he believes should be the main priority of Christian ministers and educators:

> There is no greater need in our time than that those who teach religion should concern themselves, not with tightening up the machinery, developing organization, or arranging more meetings; but rather to make Jesus real to men; to invite them into that transforming fellowship which cannot be proved save by personal experience, but which, when realized, brings men that glorious exhilaration, that sense of ineffable peace, and that escape from all bondage which are promised in the New Testament.[1]

I find support in this quote for the idea that the experience of an intimate, interactive relationship with Jesus is crucial to the Christian life and that the greatest thing any Christian preacher or teacher can do for those who will listen is to encourage them to engage in a serious pursuit of such a relationship.

And yet M. Robert Mulholland Jr., in his book *Invitation to a Journey: A Road Map for Spiritual Formation,* warns of "superficial pop spiritualities" that promise heaven on earth but produce "only failure and frustration for those genuinely hungering and thirsting after God."[2] Mulholland comments on the effect that living in an instant-gratification culture can have upon our spiritual journey:

> It is not surprising that we, as members of an instant-gratification culture, tend to become impatient with any process of development that requires of us more than a limited involvement of our time and energies. If we do not receive the desired results almost instantly, we become impatient and frustrated.
>
> Often our spiritual quest becomes a search for the right technique, the proper method, the perfect program that can immediately deliver the desired results of spiritual maturity and wholeness. Or we try to create the atmosphere for the "right" spiritual moment, the "perfect" setting in which God can touch us into instantaneous wholeness. If only we can find the right trick, the right book or the right guru, go to the right retreat, hear the right sermon, instantly we will be transformed into a new person at a new level of spirituality and wholeness.[3]

These sobering words rightfully warn us to avoid any approach to Christian spirituality that promises to be easy or to provide instantaneous results. I'm hopeful, however, that no one reading *Christ's Empowering Presence* will make the mistake of concluding that "the pursuit" is some sort of trick or gimmick—just another superficial pop spirituality that can't really deliver the goods.

I've argued in these pages that the daily habit of maintaining a sense of ongoing spiritual communion with the risen Christ really can produce a "Colossians 3 kind of life" and, therefore, is at the very heart of Christian spirituality. I've attempted to help my readers (a) gain a *vision* of what this particular spiritual exercise involves (part one), (b) form a sturdy *intention* to engage in it (part two), and (c) become aware of the various *means* by which this all-important intention can be carried out (part three).

Toward these three ends, we've surveyed what many of the greatest spiritual masters in the history of Christian spirituality (ancient and contemporary) have had to say about the nature and benefits of this particular spiritual formation practice, along with their specific suggestions on how it should be employed. We were also careful to scour the Scriptures (Old and New Testaments), looking for any sign that the Spirit who inspired them does indeed have an interest in our learning to practice the presence of God. Finally, I've also provided, though genuinely reluctant to do so, a transparent description of a typical day in my own life and the role that an earnest engagement in "the pursuit" plays in it.

All along the way I've endeavored to make clear that I'm still a long way off from being the perfect example of someone fully formed in the image of Christ. (So if anyone is looking for an approach to spirituality that provides immediate results, this isn't it.) At the same time, I've also pointed out that I've seen enough progress along the way to keep me engaged in the *process*—to keep me on the path of this spiritual journey toward an increasingly intimate, interactive relationship with God through Jesus Christ.

All of this is to say that, while I fully recognize how one might be tempted to view the subject of this book as just another superficial pop spirituality, for the reasons presented above I hope you won't come to that conclusion. The pursuit of Christ's empowering presence is not some trick or gimmick. It's the honest-to-goodness key to a "Colossians 3 kind of life," and it lies at the very heart of Christian spirituality!

And yet I dare not bring this book to a close without reminding us that the spiritual exercise put forward in these pages *can* be turned into a mere *method* or *technique,* if we ever forget that its goal is a real *relationship* with a sovereign God rather than some sort of pious persona presented to others. Though it's possible to turn "the pursuit" into something we can manage in our own strength, on our own terms, and for our own reasons, this must never be—not if we are sincere about being formed in the image of Christ.

In his book *A Cry for Mercy: Prayers from the Genesee,* Henri Nouwen confesses in the following prayer his radical need for God to be not only genuinely responsive to him but also, at times, to actually take the initiative toward authentic encounter, lest all of his attempts at spiritual growth prove vain:

> Listen, O Lord, to my prayers. Listen to my desire to be with you, to dwell in your house, and to let my whole being be filled with your presence. But none of this is possible without you. When you are not the one who fills me, I am soon filled with endless thoughts and concerns that divide me and tear me away from you. Even thoughts about you, good spiritual thoughts, can be little more than distractions when you are not their author.
>
> O Lord, thinking about you, being fascinated with theological ideas and discussions, being excited about histories of Christian spirituality and stimulated by thoughts and ideas about prayer and meditation, all of this can be as much an expression of greed as the unruly desire for food, possessions, or power.
>
> Every day I see again that only you can teach me to pray, only you can set my heart at rest, only you can let me dwell in your presence. No book, no idea, no concept or theory will ever bring me close to you unless you yourself are the one who lets these instruments become the way to you.
>
> But Lord, let me at least remain open to your initiative; let me wait patiently and attentively for that hour when you will come and break through all the walls I have erected. Teach me, O Lord, to pray. Amen.[4]

I couldn't have said it better. Real relationships are messy and impossible to "manage." Genuine Christian spirituality involves a real relationship with a sovereign God who can't be made to perform upon command. Ultimately, we can't control the degree to which our spirituality will include real encounters with the living God. As I ponder Nouwen's prayer, I hear within it a gentle call for all who would take their spirituality seriously to learn the value of *humility, honesty, trust,* and *perseverance.*

Years ago I ran across a story-poem that wonderfully portrays the need for Christ-followers to possess these four virtues. Appropriately, the poem pictures this life as a long, exciting, and sometimes scary journey experienced in partnership with the risen Christ. On more than one occasion over the years the concepts communicated through this quirky poetic piece have inspired me to stay the course, despite the thick clouds of spiritual ambiguity that sometimes (often) fill my field of vision. I can think of no better way to conclude a book devoted to the theme of cultivating an ongoing sense of Christ's empowering presence than to make you aware of this delightful description of the adventure that is at the heart of genuine Christian discipleship. After you read it, I trust you'll agree.

The Road of Life

At first I saw God as my observer,
my judge,
keeping track of the things I did wrong,
so as to know whether I merited heaven
or hell when I die.
He was out there sort of like a president.
I recognized
His picture when I saw it,
but I really didn't know Him.

But later on,
when I met Christ,
it seemed as though life were rather like a bike ride,
but it was a tandem bike,
and I noticed that Christ
was in the back helping me pedal.

I don't know when it was
that He suggested that we change places,
but life has not been the same since.

When I had control,
I knew the way.
It was rather boring,
but predictable . . .
It was the shortest distance between two points.

But when He took the lead,
He knew delightful long cuts,
up mountains,
and through rocky places
at breakneck speeds,
it was all I could do to hang on!
Even though it looked like madness,
He said, "Pedal!"

I worried and was anxious
and asked,
"Where are you taking me?"
He laughed and didn't answer,
and I started to learn to trust.

I forgot my boring life
and entered into the adventure.

And when I'd say "I'm scared,"
He'd lean back and touch my hand.

He took me to people with gifts that I needed,
gifts of healing,
acceptance
and joy.
They gave me gifts to take on my journey,
my Lord's and mine.

And we were off again.
He said, "Give the gifts away; they're extra baggage, too
much weight."
So I did,
to the people we met,
and I found that in giving I received,
and still our burden was light.

I did not trust Him,
at first,
in control of my life.
I thought He'd wreck it;
but he knows bike secrets,
knows how to make it bend to take sharp corners,
knows how to jump to clear high rocks,
knows how to fly to shorten scary passages.

And I am learning to shut up
and pedal
in the strangest places,
and I'm beginning to enjoy the view
and the cool breeze on my face
with my delightful constant companion, Jesus Christ.

And when I'm sure I just can't do any more,
He just smiles and says . . . "Pedal!"

~ Author unknown[5]

I wish for you God's very best as you continue your own spiritual journey—a journey that I hope will involve a serious, enthusiastic pursuit of Christ's empowering presence. I encourage you to never, ever give up on the idea that it really is possible to cultivate an ongoing communion with the risen Christ and, in the process, to get closer and closer to a "Colossians 3 kind of life." After all, deep down inside . . . you know you want this! Right?

ENDNOTES

Introduction

1 Augustine, *Confessions* (New York: Oxford University Press, 1998), 3.

2 Jerry Adler, "In Search of the Spiritual," *Newsweek,* August 29, 2005, http://www.newsweek.com/id/147035.

3 For example, see Dallas Willard, *Renovation of the Heart: Putting on the Character of Christ* (Colorado Springs: NavPress, 2002), 241.

4 It's important for me, personally, to be convinced that the spiritual life practice I advocate in this book possesses genuine scriptural support. While I find inspirational value in many of the works of the spiritual masters, I do not accord any of these writings a canonical status. In other words, I am committed to *evaluating* any statement found in the corpus of devotional literature in the light of Scripture. Furthermore, my operating assumption is that, since the spiritual classics do not claim to be directly inspired by God, we are free to disagree with some statements made by them while finding great value in others, to the degree that they comport with our admittedly imperfect understanding of Scripture.

5 Willard, *Renovation of the Heart,* 85.

6 Dallas Willard, *Knowing Christ Today: Why We Can Trust Spiritual Knowledge* (New York: HarperOne, 2009), 157. Although it has become customary to refer to authors of classic books related to the spiritual life as "masters," this is not a designation they would have given themselves. We have every reason to believe that the spiritual "masters" were humble men

and women who fully recognized the degree of their spiritual imperfections, and they surely would have considered any claim to have *mastered* the spiritual life to be a very unspiritual thing for a follower of Christ to do.

7   As cited in Tim Hansel, *When I Relax I Feel Guilty* (Elgin, IL: David C. Cook Publishing, 1979), 49.

8   In his book *Invitation to a Journey: A Road Map for Spiritual Formation* (Downers Grove, IL: InterVarsity, 1993), M. Robert Mulholland Jr. makes the important point that a truly healthy Christian spirituality won't simply be about us, but will make us a force for God in the lives of others. See 40–44, 141–68.

Chapter 1

1   Dallas Willard, *Knowing Christ Today: Why We Can Trust Spiritual Knowledge* (New York: HarperOne, 2009), 157.

2   "Brother Lawrence: Practitioner of God's Presence," ChristianHistory.net, August 8, 2008, http://www.christianitytoday.com/ch/131christians/innertravelers/brotherlawrence.html.

3   Brother Lawrence, *The Practice of the Presence of God with Spiritual Maxims* (Grand Rapids: Revell, 1967), 66–67.

4   Brother Lawrence, *The Practice of the Presence of God* (Springdale, PA: Whitaker House, 1982), 12.

5   Ibid., 23.

6   Ibid., 81–82.

7   Ibid., 82–83.

8   Ibid., 19.

9   Actually, the original English translation reads: "That many do not advance in the Christian progress because they stick in penances and particular exercises, while they neglect the love of God, which is the *end*." See Brother Lawrence, *The Practice of the Presence of God with Spiritual Maxims,* 24.

10 Brother Lawrence, *The Practice of the Presence of God,* 21–22.

11 Ibid., 24.

12 Ibid., 33–34.

13 Ibid., 41.

14 Brother Lawrence, *The Practice of the Presence of God with Spiritual Maxims,* 23.

15 Ibid., 26.

16 Brother Lawrence, *The Practice of the Presence of God,* 24–25.

17 Ibid., 61.

18 Ibid., 41.

19 Ibid., 90.

20 Ibid., 83.

21 Brother Lawrence, *The Practice of the Presence of God with Spiritual Maxims*, 89–90.

22 Ibid., 90–91.

23 Ibid., 30.

24 Brother Lawrence, *The Practice of the Presence of God,* 49.

Chapter 2

1   Brent Curtis and John Eldredge, *The Sacred Romance: Drawing Closer to the Heart of God* (Nashville: Thomas Nelson, 1997), 45.

2   Richard J. Woods, *Christian Spirituality: God's Presence through the Ages* (Maryknoll, NY: Orbis, 2006), xix.

3   Ibid., 4.

4   Ibid., 7.

5   Ibid., 3.

6   Ibid.

7   See Gary Tyra, *Defeating Pharisaism: Recovering Jesus' Disciple-Making Method* (Colorado Springs: Paternoster, 2009), 124, 155, 159, 163, 251. I am indebted to Dallas Willard for the idea that Jesus possessed an "intimate, interactive" relationship with God and desired to teach his disciples how to do likewise.

8   Woods, *Christian Spirituality,* 16–17.

9   Ibid., 63.

10 Henri Nouwen, *The Way of the Heart* (Toronto: Ballantine Books, 1981), 14.

11 Ibid., 17.

12 Ibid.

13 Henri Nouwen, *Making All Things New* (San Francisco: HarperSanFrancisco, 1981), 79–80.

14 Bonaventure, *The Life of St. Francis* (Mahwah, NJ: Paulist Press, 1978), 262–63.

15 Ibid., 263–64. Note: *Cant.* is an abbreviation for the Old Testament book Canticles, also known as Song of Songs or Song of Solomon.

16 Thomas à Kempis, *The Imitation of Christ* (London: Penguin, 1952), 77.

17 Ibid., 67–68.

18 See John 15:13–15.

19 See the following passages, all of which picture the church as the bride of Christ: John 3:29; Revelation 19:7; 21:2, 9; 22:17.

20 George Lane, *Christian Spirituality* (Chicago: Loyola Press, 1984), 39.

21 Ibid., 46.

22 Ibid., 46–47.

23 Francis de Sales, *Introduction to the Devout Life* (New York: Doubleday, 1966), 10.

24 Ibid., 84.

25 Ibid., 96.

26 Ibid., 99.

27 Ibid., 153.

28 Jeremy Taylor, "Holy Living" in *Selected Writings,* ed. C. H. Sisson (Manchester, England: Carcanet Press Limited, 1990), 61–62.

Chapter 3

1 Dallas Willard, *Knowing Christ Today: Why We Can Trust Spiritual Knowledge* (New York: HarperOne, 2009), 157.

2 Frank C. Laubach, *Letters by a Modern Mystic* (Syracuse: New Readers Press, 1979), as cited in Frank C. Laubach, *Man of Prayer: Selected Writings of a World Missionary* (Syracuse: Laubach Literacy International, 1990), 20.

3 Frank C. Laubach, *Prayer: The Mightiest Force in the World,* as cited in Laubach, *Man of Prayer,* 245.

4 A. W. Tozer, *The Pursuit of God* (Camp Hill, PA: Christian Publications, 1993), 84.

5 Ibid., 89–90.

6 Leslie Weatherhead, *The Transforming Friendship* (Nashville: Abingdon, 1977), 18.

7 Ibid., 7–8.

8 Ibid., 29.

9 Ibid., 35.

10 Ibid., 45.

11 Spiritual formation authority M. Robert Mulholland Jr. writes: "The journey of faith, the path to spiritual wholeness, lies in our increasingly faithful response to the One whose purpose shapes our path, whose grace redeems our detours, whose power liberates us from the crippling bondages of our previous journey, and whose transforming presence meets us at each turn in our road. Holistic spirituality is a pilgrimage of deepening responsiveness to God's control of our life and being." I like what this quote says about the sovereignty of God as it relates to our spiritual health: a truly vibrant spirituality is not something we can create apart from God's purpose, grace, power, and *transforming presence.* The way of Christian discipleship is a prolonged pilgrimage of *deepening responsiveness* and a lifelong journey of *increasingly faithful responses* to what God is up to in our lives, not something we are ultimately in control of. See M. Robert Mulholland Jr., *Invitation to a Journey: A Road Map for Spiritual Formation*

(Downers Grove, IL: InterVarsity, 1993), 168. I address this theme again in the conclusion of *Christ's Empowering Presence.*

12 Willard, *Knowing Christ Today,* 156.

13 Ibid., 159.

14 Ibid., 161.

15 Dallas Willard, *Renovation of the Heart: Putting on the Character of Christ* (Colorado Springs: NavPress, 2002), 31.

16 Ibid., 106.

17 Ibid., 112.

18 Ibid., 42–43.

19 Ibid., 51.

20 Ibid., 241–42.

21 Dallas Willard, *Hearing God: Developing a Conversational Relationship with God* (Downers Grove, IL: InterVarsity, 1999), 10.

22 Ibid., 18.

23 Ibid., 22.

24 Jan Johnson, *Enjoying the Presence of God* (Colorado Springs: NavPress, 1996), 14.

25 Richard Foster, *Prayer: Finding the Heart's True Home* (San Francisco: HarperSanFrancisco, 1992), 119.

26 Ibid.

27 Foster, *Prayer,* 119. Foster notes that, in order, the quotations are from the following sources: Brother Lawrence, *The Practice of the Presence of God* (Philadelphia: Judson, n.d.), 60; *Writings from the Philokalia on Prayer of the Heart,* trans. E. Kadloubovsky and G. E. H. Palmer (London: Faber & Faber, 1975), 85; Julian of Norwich, *Showings,* trans. Edmund Colledge and James Walsh (New York: Paulist Press, 1978), 253; *On the Prayer of Jesus: From the Ascetic Essays of Bishop Ignatius Brianchaninov,* trans. Father Lazarus (London: John W. Watkins, 1965), 60; Gloria Hutchinson, *Six Ways to Pray from Six Great Saints* (Cincinnati: St. Anthony Messenger Press, 1982), 10; Laubach, *Letters by a Modern Mystic,* 23.

28 Foster, *Prayer,* 124–25. Thomas Kelly, *A Testament of Devotion* (New York: Harper and Row, 1941), 35.

29 John Ortberg, *The Life You've Always Wanted: Spiritual Disciplines for Ordinary People* (Grand Rapids: Zondervan, 1997).

30 John Ortberg, *God Is Closer Than You Think: This Can Be the Greatest Moment of Your Life Because This Moment Is the Place Where You Can Meet God* (Grand Rapids: Zondervan, 2005), 14.

31 Ibid., 23–24.

32 Ortberg, *God Is Closer Than You Think*, 25–26. Brother Lawrence, *The Practice of the Presence of God* (Springdale, PA: Whitaker House, 1982), 61.

33 Ortberg, *God Is Closer Than You Think*, 38–39. William Barry, *Finding God in All Things* (Notre Dame, IN: Ave Maria Press, 1991), 14–15.

34 Ortberg, *God Is Closer Than You Think*, 55.

Chapter 4

1 Richard Foster, *Prayer* (San Francisco: HarperSanFrancisco, 1992), 1.

2 Richard J. Woods, *Christian Spirituality: God's Presence through the Ages* (Maryknoll, NY: Orbis, 2006), 5.

3 Ibid., 4–5.

4 Ibid., 6.

5 For a more thorough study of the theme of God's presence in the Psalms, see Samuel Terrien, *The Elusive Presence: Toward a New Biblical Theology* (New York: Harper and Row, 1978), 278–349.

6 See William Law, *A Serious Call to a Devout and Holy Life* (New York: Paulist Press, 1978), 209, 224; Dietrich Bonhoeffer, *Life Together* (San Francisco: HarperSanFrancisco, 1954), 44–50; Tarsicius J. Van Bavel, *The Rule of Saint Augustine* (Kalamazoo, MI: Cistercian Publications, 1984), 13, 62; Anthony C. Meisel and M. L. del Mastro, *The Rule of St. Benedict* (New York: Doubleday, 1975,) 68.

7 The law of Moses mandated that all Israelite men make three pilgrimages each year to worship before the Lord at the temple in Jerusalem (see Exodus 23:14, 17; 34:23; Deuteronomy 16:16). While the author of Psalm 84 no doubt had such literal journeys in mind, followers of Christ can and should approach each and every day, figuratively speaking, with our hearts "set on pilgrimage"!

8 See Dallas Willard, *Spirit of the Disciplines: Understanding How God Changes Lives* (San Francisco: HarperSanFrancisco, 1988), 108–10, for a discussion of the realism of biblical language. Though we must not interpret Scripture in a manner that is overly literal, neither should we rush to an overly figurative, symbolic, and metaphorical interpretation. Thus, when we read of the actions taken by a psalmist to experience God's presence, our default should be to take him seriously, actually endeavoring to follow his example in as literal a manner as possible, using common sense as our guide.

Chapter 5

1 For example, in Matthew 6:3–4, 6, 17–18, Jesus instructs his followers to practice their piety in a way that takes God's real presence in their lives seriously.

This theme shows up again in the tutorial on prayer presented by Jesus in the same chapter (Matthew 6:9–13). When you think of it, the Lord's Prayer presumes largely upon the idea that Christians are actually conversing with a loving heavenly Father who can be counted on to invade our present circumstances, responding to our petitions for things such as provision, protection, and personal guidance. It's clear from these and other passages that one of Jesus' main messages to his disciples was that they could and should cultivate their own intimate, interactive relationship with God the Father.

2 Indeed, because Paul's letters contain the phrase "in Christ" no less than eighty-three times, some New Testament scholars give attention to something they refer to as his "in Christ" mysticism. This is the idea that, according to Paul, Christian spirituality absolutely hinges upon the believer understanding that he or she lives his or her life in this present age "in Christ." An acknowledgment of such a Pauline concept lends support for the thesis of this chapter, that "the pursuit" is a spiritual life practice supported by authors of the New Testament.

Chapter 6

1 For an excellent discussion of the "hurry sickness" and how we might develop a spirituality that mitigates it, see John Ortberg, *The Life You've Always Wanted* (Grand Rapids: Zondervan, 1997), 81–96.

2 Brother Lawrence, *The Practice of the Presence of God with Spiritual Maxims* (Grand Rapids: Fleming H. Revell, 1967), 35–36.

3 Ibid., 71.

4 Ibid., 71–72.

5 Ibid., 72.

6 Thomas à Kempis, *The Imitation of Christ* (London: Penguin, 1952), 76.

7 Frank C. Laubach, *Man of Prayer: Selected Writings of a World Missionary* (Syracuse: Laubach Literacy International, 1990), 21.

8 Ibid., 27.

9 Ibid., 31.

10 A. W. Tozer, *The Pursuit of God* (Camp Hill, PA: Christian Publications, 1993), 85.

11 Ibid., 90.

12 Leslie Weatherhead, *The Transforming Friendship* (Nashville: Abingdon, 1977), 35.

13 Richard Foster, *Prayer* (San Francisco: HarperSanFrancisco, 1992), 121.

14 Dallas Willard, *Renovation of the Heart: Putting on the Character of Christ* (Colorado Springs: NavPress, 2002), 14.

15 Ibid., 21–22.

16 Ibid., 20.

17 Ibid., 14.

18 Ibid., 19.

19 Willard, *Renovation of the Heart*, 19–20. See also M. Robert Mulholland Jr., *Invitation to a Journey: A Road Map for Spiritual Formation* (Downers Grove, IL: InterVarsity, 1993), 23.

20 Willard, *Renovation of the Heart*, 22.

21 Ibid., 241.

22 Ibid., 218.

23 Ibid., 15 (italics added).

24 Ibid.

25 Ibid., 23 (italics added).

26 Ibid., 25.

27 Ibid., 30.

28 Ibid., 31.

29 Ibid., 218.

30 Ibid., 112–13.

31 Ibid., 82.

32 Ibid., 109.

33 Please see Willard's *Renovation of the Heart* (218–21) for an extended discussion of the effects that our living a God-intoxicated life will have upon our thought life, feelings, choices, body, social context, and soul. Willard refers to this section as "A Composite Portrait of 'Children of Light.'" I find it to be an informative and moving treatment of the benefits of "the pursuit." Much too long to cite in this work, this section alone is worth the price of Willard's book!

Chapter 7

1 Charles Wells Moulton, *The Library of Literary Criticism of English and American Authors, Vol. 8: 1639–1729* (Charleston, SC: Nabu Press, 2010), 211.

2 Jeremy Taylor, "Holy Living" in *Selected Writings,* ed. C. H. Sisson (Manchester, England: Carcanet Press Limited, 1990), 62.

3 Ibid., 62–63.

4 I've found that one sign that I'm truly conversing with God, rather than merely talking at him, is that my prayer utterances begin to take the form of questions I put to God, rather than statements I direct at him. For example, "Lord, what are you up to in my life right now?" "How am I supposed to respond to this or that situation?" "How should I pray for this or that person, given what he or she is going through?" These are the kinds of questions I find myself putting to God when my prayer times are marked by a serious realization of his real presence.

5 *Jeremy Taylor: Selected Writings*, 63.

6 Ibid.

7 Ibid., 63–64. Genesis 5:22–24 says that Enoch "walked with God" three hundred years and "then he was no more, because God took him away" (i.e., to God's presence without experiencing death).

8 Ibid., 64.

9 Ibid.

10 I'm absolutely convinced that an ongoing experience of Christ's real presence in our lives can't help but produce within us a greater compunction to address the needs of the poor and hurting, who exist all around us.

11 *Jeremy Taylor: Selected Writings*, 64.

12 Ibid.

13 Ibid., 65.

Chapter 8

1 Simon Tugwell, *Prayer* (Dublin, Ireland: Veritas, 1975); cited in Brent Curtis and John Eldredge, *The Sacred Romance* (Nashville: Thomas Nelson, 1997), 69, 81.

2 Jan Johnson, *Enjoying the Presence of God* (Colorado Springs: NavPress, 1996), 134.

3 See Gary Tyra, *Defeating Pharisaism: Recovering Jesus' Disciple-Making Method* (Colorado Springs: Paternoster, 2009).

4 John Ortberg, *The Life You've Always Wanted: Spiritual Disciplines for Ordinary People* (Grand Rapids: Zondervan, 1997), 196.

5 Ibid., 197.

6 Ibid., 197–98.

7 Francis de Sales, *Introduction to the Devout Life* (New York: Doubleday, 1966), 81.

8 De Sales offers his readers four methods by which they might "place themselves in God's presence." Paraphrased, these four methods are (1) Reflect upon the fact that God is everywhere around you; (2) Reflect upon the fact that God lives in your heart, your spirit; (3) Reflect upon the fact that Christ, who sits at the right hand of God in heaven, is constantly watching over his people; (4) Use your imagination when in prayer and worship, picturing Christ next to you. Ibid., 84–85.

9 Ibid., 82.

10 Ibid., 91.

11 Ibid., 97.

12 Ibid., 98–99.

13 Ibid., 153.

14 Ibid., 161.

15 Frank C. Laubach, *Man of Prayer: Selected Writings of a World Missionary* (Syracuse: Laubach Literacy International, 1990), 11.

16 Ibid., 31.

17 Ibid., 195.

18 Ibid.

19 Ibid., 204.

20 At the same time, the last thing I want to do in a book such as this is promote a triumphalistic approach to Christian spirituality that doesn't adequately grapple with the fact that there are times when, no matter how sincere we are before God, our lives seem devoid of Christ's presence (empowering or otherwise). Though divine discipline is a reality, we should never allow the evil one to succeed in tempting us to conclude that these days of *spiritual desolation* (as Thomas à Kempis might refer to them) are somehow unique to us and an indication of our having been abandoned by God. It seems that all believers experience what St. John of the Cross referred to as the "dark night of the soul"—not simply because we're all sinners, but because God in his unfathomable wisdom appears to use these days of desolation to cause us to engage in the deep reflection necessary for the next leg in our spiritual journey. In other words, it's a growth thing. With this painful reality in mind, here is some excellent counsel from the pen of Richard Foster:

"I would like to offer one more counsel to those who find themselves devoid of the presence of God. It is this: wait on God. Wait, silent and still. Wait, attentive and responsive. Learn that trust precedes faith. Faith is a little like putting your car into gear, and right now you cannot exercise faith, you cannot move forward. Do not berate yourself for this. But when you are unable to put your spiritual life into drive, do not put it into reverse; put it into neutral. Trust is how you put your spiritual life in neutral. Trust is confidence in the character of God. Firmly and deliberately you say, 'I do not understand what God is doing or even where God is, but I know that he is out to do me good.' This is trust. This is how to wait.

"I do not fully understand the reasons for the wildernesses of God's absence. This I do know: while the wilderness is necessary, it is never meant to be permanent. In God's time and in God's way the desert will give way to a land flowing with milk and honey. And as we wait for that promised land of the soul, we can echo the prayer of Bernard of Clairvaux, 'O my God, deep calls unto deep (Psalm 42:7).

The deep of my profound misery calls to the deep of Your infinite mercy.'" (From Richard Foster, *Prayer* [San Francisco: HarperSanFrancisco, 1992], 24.)

21 For an excellent discussion of the importance of cultivating a spirituality that is both corporate and social, see the chapters devoted to these two themes in M. Robert Mulholland Jr.'s book, *Invitation to a Journey: A Road Map for Spiritual Formation* (Downers Grove, IL: InterVarsity, 1993), 143–68.

22 Jan Johnson, *Enjoying the Presence of God* (Colorado Springs: NavPress, 1996), 21.

23 Ibid., 30.

24 Ibid., 22–23.

25 Ibid., 23.

26 de Sales, *Introduction to the Devout Life,* 184.

27 John Ortberg, *God Is Closer Than You Think: This Can Be the Greatest Moment of Your Life Because This Moment Is the Place Where You Can Meet God* (Grand Rapids: Zondervan, 2005), 72.

28 Ibid.

29 Ibid., 76.

30 Ibid.

31 Ibid., 80.

32 Ibid., 75.

33 Ibid., 78.

34 Ibid., 79.

35 Dallas Willard, *Renovation of the Heart: Putting on the Character of Christ* (Colorado Springs: NavPress, 2002), 70.

36 Ibid., 112–13.

37 Ibid., 221.

38 Ibid., 114.

Chapter 9

1 John Ortberg, "Your Spiritual Growth Plan," *Leadership Journal* 31:1 (2010), 83.

2 Ibid., 82.

3 As beneficial as I find it to begin my days with a fairly involved "quiet time," I fully recognize that it's possible to become centered in Christ in a much less complex manner. For a variety of reasons (e.g., work schedule, body rhythms, and so forth), it may be difficult or less efficient for some to engage in the kind of morning exercises I describe here. Though the spiritual masters we've looked at are fairly unanimous in stating the importance of spending just a few moments each morning becoming centered in Christ, surely it's possible to maintain an

intimate level of communion with Jesus while conducting a formal "quiet time" either less frequently or at some other time during the day. Thus, I encourage all my readers to feel the freedom to transpose the concepts presented here into a devotional routine that works for them.

4   Frank C. Laubach, *Man of Prayer: Selected Writings of a World Missionary* (Syracuse: Laubach Literacy International, 1990), 199.

5   Once again, if your particular life situation makes such a practice impossible, don't fret; simply make use of any open spaces in your daily schedule to do your best to connect with Christ in a similar manner. For instance, my wife routinely turns her daily train ride to and from downtown Los Angeles into an opportunity to "walk" with the Lord, figuratively speaking.

6   Please see Gary and Patti Tyra, *Beyond the Bliss: Discovering Your Uniqueness in Marriage* (Colorado Springs: Biblica Publishing, 2010).

Conclusion

1   Leslie Weatherhead, *The Transforming Friendship* (Nashville: Abingdon, 1977), 37.

2   M. Robert Mulholland Jr., *Invitation to a Journey: A Road Map for Spiritual Formation* (Downers Grove, IL: InterVarsity, 1993), 11.

3   Ibid., 20.

4   Henri Nouwen, *A Cry for Mercy: Prayers from the Genesee* (New York: Random House, 2002), 27–28.

5   Cited in Tim Hansel, *Holy Sweat* (Waco: Word, 1987), 51–53.

ALSO AVAILABLE

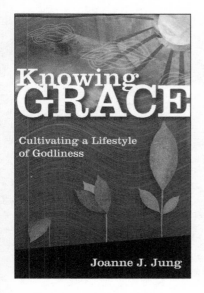

We've read books and heard sermons on drawing near to, enjoying, and being intimate with God, yet all this seems so far from our reality. Why is that? Perhaps part of the problem is that it feels so dutiful, and that gets in the way of truly knowing him.

How can we move from duty to delight? *Knowing Grace* fosters and deepens the reader's engagement with God by emphasizing his initiating, inviting, and empowering us to engage with him in ways that foster a greater sensitivity to his movements, stirrings, nudges, and voice. By growing more familiar with being in his presence, we experience more of his grace, which moves us from duty to delight.

Paperback, 208 pages, 5.5 x 8.5
ISBN: 978-1-60657-090-6
Retail: $15.99

Available for purchase at book retailers everywhere.

Christians who think simplistically often imagine sin is a problem only for unbelievers, yet reality clearly points to its looming presence in our lives and its deadly impact on the church. By not openly admitting and addressing the sin in our lives, we deceive ourselves; and the world looking on is misled through this hypocrisy. *Spiritual Formation* is a scalpel to cut away tumors of ignorance, avoidance, and pride, creating honest believers who then will be an authentic witness to a hurting world.

Paperback, 224 pages, 6 x 9
ISBN: 978-1-93406-882-3
Retail: $19.99

Available for purchase at book retailers everywhere.